WHY ARE THERE MONKEYS?

WHY ARE THERE MONKEYS?

(and other questions for God)

BROOKE JONES

LUMINARE PRESS
WWW.LUMINAREPRESS.COM

Disclaimer: Any breaches of Grammatical Etiquette or proper punctuation in this book have been intentionally committed by me (the author). The fine folks at Luminare Press did their best to correct my flagrant violations, but to no avail. I insisted on my right to be wrong. There is, in fact, a method to my madness, and I eagerly await correspondence from any reader who recognizes my perversity and sees it for what it actually is. —Brooke Jones

Printed in the United States of America

Luminare Press
442 Charnelton St.
Eugene, OR 97401
www.luminarepress.com

LCCN: 2020921013
ISBN: 978-1-64388-464-6

For my Wabi Sabi

&

For Faith, lost & found

CONTENTS

Prologue 1

Introduction 3

CHAPTER 1
And Now for Something Completely
Different 7

CHAPTER 2
Monty Hall, the Pope, and the Wicked
Witch of the East 10

CHAPTER 3
Why Are There Monkeys? 15

CHAPTER 4
Close Encounters of the Third
Cousin Kind 33

CHAPTER 5
I'll Take Gibberish for $800, Alex 38

CHAPTER 6
Take Two Troglodytes and Call Me
in the Morning 41

CHAPTER 7
Christians, Muslims, and Jews,
Oh My! 48

CHAPTER 8
Faith, Dope, and Clarity or Three
Million Men Named Jesus 56

CHAPTER 9
Kiss My Ass or Miracles, Mets,
and Mules 61

CHAPTER 10
People, People Who See Dead People. 66

CHAPTER 11
Will the Real Marie Antoinette
Please Stay Dead 69

CHAPTER 12
Of Mice and Menageries 72

CHAPTER 13
And Why Were You Born? 76

CHAPTER 14
My Karma Ran Over My Dogma 79

CHAPTER 15
Don't Sin Under the Apple Tree. 82

CHAPTER 16
How Much Is That Pony in the Closet? 86

CHAPTER 17
If He's Ugly, Stupid, and Rude,
He's Probably Not the Devil 90

CHAPTER 18
A Rabbi, a Priest, and a Monk
Walk into A 93

CHAPTER 19
Tonight on the Late Show—Dead
People Cook Dinner 97

CHAPTER 20
Just Because It's Free Doesn't
Mean It Won't Cost You 101

CHAPTER 21
Is That Your Final Question? 105

Epilogue 112

Acknowledgments 121

About the Author 123

PROLOGUE

Eternal, all powerful, all knowing—according to the authors of *Webster's Unabridged Dictionary*, these are the primary attributes of God. Of course, according to these same authors, *timidity, mildness, and weakness* are the primary attributes of women, so I take what said authors say with a pound and a half of salt....but that has nothing whatever to do with my story.

I spent several decades not at all convinced that there actually was a God, but it wasn't a subject to which I paid much attention. I was what you might refer to as a '*Closet Agnostic*'. This agnostic lack of conviction did not, however, prevent me from routinely mentioning His name whenever I overslept, slammed my finger in a door, or got arrested...but we won't go into that at the moment.

This lack of conviction also did not prevent me from occasionally crossing my fingers and toes and hoping (I said hoping, not praying—the concept of a praying Agnostic is too weird, even for me) that if He did exist, in addition to His other benevolent attributes, He would have the ability to laugh.

On those rare occasions when the thought of God did appear in my consciousness, I found myself thinking about the existence of Heaven. That thought led me to the realization that if there was a Heaven, I might want to go there someday (as opposed to going to that *other* place located somewhere significantly south of South)...and therein lies the rub.

You see, due to the rather unorthodox life I had been living, I stood absolutely no chance of walking through those proverbial Pearly Gates, unless the Man in Charge had the most bizarre sense of humor in the Cosmos. Now I ask you, what are the odds of *that*?

INTRODUCTION

It started with drugs. I'm a child of the Sixties. For me, everything started with drugs. It was just another in a long line of sad, sorry, self-indulgent nights, no different than any other…until…

They say they struggled to bring me back. They did everything they knew how to do. They held me under a cold shower. They slapped me. They slapped me again. They said they slapped, and slapped, and then they slapped some more. At some point, they were slapping me primarily to vent their rage at my stupidity. It made them feel a bit better, but it didn't do a thing for me. I was beyond their rage, because I was dead.

One minute I was alive—the next minute I was dead. Drugs can do that to you, but I'm getting ahead of myself.

It was 1950. Harry Truman was president. Everyone wore hats.

I was born into a Jewish family. Jewish families come in three varieties. There are Reform Jews,

Conservative Jews and Orthodox Jews. My family was of the Reform persuasion. Reform Jews are people who cling to a tribal identity while knowing precious little about their tribal history.

For Jews of all persuasions, Yom Kippur is the holiest day of the year. It's the day set aside for what is officially referred to as the Atonement Of Sin (and unofficially recognized as a sacred excuse to visit the golf course). Every year on that day, the Reform Jews of my community, dressed to impress, attended worship services, not in the tony local temple, but at the Westchester Community Center just down the road—a place more often used by the Ringling Bros. and Barnum & Bailey Circus and the Harlem Globetrotters (the temple was just too small to hold all those mink coats).

There I would sit, hands folded in my lap, dutifully watching the Rabbi and listening to the Cantor. Unfortunately, no matter how hard I tried to focus on them, all I could see were dancing elephants, and all I could hear were dribbling basketballs. By the time I was eight years old, I had concluded that if there were such a thing as the Holy Trinity (one of my best friends was a devout Catholic), it must consist of God, Celina the Elephant Girl, and Meadowlark Lemon.

It was 1969. Richard Nixon was president.
Everyone wore hair.

I experimented with sex, drugs, Rock 'n Roll, and religion. In college, I majored in three of the four. At various times, and for various lengths of time, I was an Agnostic, an Atheist, a Rosicrucian, an Existentialist (mandatory for all freshman English Lit students), a Nihilist (mandatory for all sophomore philosophy students), and a Buddhist (mandatory for nothing, and preferred by two out of three Flower Children).

I practiced Yoga religiously, so to speak. Twice a day, I would contort myself into positions I can only fantasize about now. I treated my body like a temple, ingesting only natural products like brown rice, mushrooms, and…heroin.

It was 1975. Gerald Ford was president.
Everyone wore heels.

Was it too much of a good thing, or was it just enough of a decidedly bad thing? Either way, I was overdosing. As I lay dying, I prayed to every deity I had ever heard of, read about, or studied. I meditated on a framed picture of Swami Satchidananda. I chanted. I envisioned several Hollywood actors who had portrayed Jesus. I did everything I could think of. Then, I died.

I had never heard of "*Near Death Experiences*." For me, born and raised in and around New York City, bright lights and tunnels were nothing more than the basic ingredients of traffic jams. Imagine my surprise when I found myself *floating* in a gossamer tunnel that seemed to be made of light—a three-dimensional, pulsing, white light. A warm, three-dimensional, pulsing, white light. A warm, three-dimensional, pulsing white light that felt *alive.*

It's amazing what a dead girl can do in eight minutes. Take me, for example. I met God. I spoke to God. God spoke to me, and these are the words we shared.

CHAPTER 1

⬯

And Now for Something Completely Different

Awarm, dry fog hangs in the motionless air. I look around and realize that I haven't the slightest idea where I am, or how I got here. "Hello," I whisper. The stillness of the environment seems to call for whispers. No answer, so I repeat a bit louder, "Hello?" Again, no answer. "Hello? Hello? HELLO"? Silence. Silence. Silence. Unaccustomed as I am to being ignored, and brandishing the regrettable lack of decorum for which I am notorious, I raise my voice and say to anyone who might be lurking in the distance, "Would someone please tell me where the Hell I am!"

Instantly, the warm, foggy, motionless air fills with something that approximates lightning, and my ears fill with something that definitely sounds like thunder. I duck, and, as I hide my eyes from the lightning, the thunder becomes a Voice. "Watch your language. Try to remember where you are," the

Voice commands in a baritone that, as I think about it now, makes Darth Vader sound like Minnie Mouse…and I would have happily obliged had it not been for the fact that I don't know where I am, so it would be impossible for me to *remember* where I am…which is what leads me to reply, "I will, just as soon as I find out where I am!"

"You are at My front door," responds the disembodied Voice.

Okay, now we're getting somewhere. Where? I'm not sure, but I think I sense progress here. I'm at *somebody's* front door. (I don't see a door, but that seems to be the least of my problems.) "Just who might you be?" I challenge.

"Let's just say I Am!"

Okay, if you insist. "I am," I say obediently.

"No, *I* am," the Voice corrects.

"Right, you am, but who am you?" When I lose my syntax, I know that my sanity can't be far behind. "I'm confused," I confess.

"Most people are when they first arrive at My door."

Well, that was a lovely trip. We've just gone in a complete circle, and here we are, right back where we began, which is I still don't know where, so I try again.

"Where am I?"

Again I hear, "You are at My front door."

Getting dizzy…must sit down.

I look around for a place to sit. I don't see one. Come to think of it, I don't see anything, except that fog and that light, and then I hear the Voice say, "Welcome." Nothing elaborate, just one word, *welcome*, and that's when it hits me. "Oh my God!" I say.

"By Jove, I think she's got it," says He.

CHAPTER 2

Monty Hall, the Pope, and the Wicked Witch of the East

I'm *dead. I'm* dead. I. Am. Dead. I say it three different ways, putting a different emphasis on it each time, but it doesn't matter. Dead is dead, and I am…well…dead. I take a few deep breaths. Realizing that breathing is a rather unusual thing for a dead woman to be doing, I quickly take a few more.

My heart feels as if it's attached to the roof of my mouth. My pulse is banging in my ears like a bass drum. I close my eyes and try to concentrate, but all I can come up with is that I'm dead! I'm dead and I'm standing at God's front door! I'm dead, I'm standing at God's front door, and I'm talking to God! I would have dropped dead out of pure shock, but inasmuch as I am already dead, it occurs to me that that would be redundant.

Eventually (is it a moment or a millennium?), I'm able to catch my breath and stand up without falling over. All around me is a light—a new light. Not the light of the tunnel but a pulsating light that seems to *breathe*. When the Voice whispers, the light becomes soft. When the Voice bellows, the light becomes blinding. Despite the fact that I can't see Him, I know that I'm standing in the presence of God, but for the life of me (for the death of me?), I'm not the least bit frightened. I haven't the slightest idea why I'm not terrified, but I'm not. Maybe I'm in shock. After all, I just learned that I'm dead. That alone should be enough to shock a girl. Whatever the reason, my knees aren't knocking. My teeth aren't chattering. In fact, I feel absolutely calm and comfortable.

"What happens now?" I ask.

"What would you like to happen?" the Voice answers gently.

I consider clicking my heels together three times and saying "there's no place like home" but choose, instead, to say, "Can I go home now?"

"Some would say that you are home right now," the Voice whispers.

"Some would say that Richard Nixon was honest—what does that prove?"

"That some are even more confused than you are," He chuckles.

Well, slap my landlord and call me for breakfast—there *is* a God, and He has a sense of humor! It's amazing what a girl can learn when she's dead!

Okay, so this is Heaven. I know I should be seriously impressed, but I'm not. Maybe it's because I don't see anything. I don't mean I don't see anything impressive. I mean I don't see *anything*—as in *nothing*. There is nothing there except me and the Voice of, well, you know—God. Not that me and the Voice of God in the same place at the same time isn't the most mind-boggling thing that has ever happened to me. It's just that, well, it isn't Pearly Gates or cloud couches or whatever else I thought Heaven was supposed to be furnished with.

"So, this is Heaven," I hear myself say out loud.

"No, this is My front door," He says again, adding, "Heaven is on the other side of My door."

Well, that explains it. I'm not seeing the furnished unit. I'm standing outside, on the stoop. The porch. The doorstep. Whatever.

Speaking in a voice so timid that I almost don't recognize it, I say, "I probably don't belong here, but may I come in?" I don't know what I expected. Maybe "after the life you've led? You must be kidding!" followed by the earsplitting laughter of the Heavenly Host. Something along those lines. I am definitely *not* expecting the response I receive.

"We'll see," says the Voice.

I can't believe my ears. God just quoted the Wicked Witch of the East, also known as my mother. It is more than a girl can bear! "Please don't say that!" I beg. (Well, okay, I whine.)

"Why not?"

"Because that's my mother's favorite expression, and when she says it, it always means *NO*."

"I am *not* your mother" He says.

"Thank God for that!" I reply, momentarily forgetting where I am.

"You are quite welcome."

A wave of Cosmic irony washes over me. I look down. (Stands to reason, doesn't it? If I'm at Heaven's door, Earth *must* be below me, right?) "Hey Mom," I shout, "you think I'll be calling you this Sunday? We'll see!" I laugh. Then I laugh some more. I'm dead, and I'm laughing. Who knew?

When I finally stop laughing, I realize that God has been laughing right along with me. The sound of His laughter is unlike anything I have ever experienced. It roars like a lion and purrs like a kitten, all at the same time. It doesn't ring in my ears—it vibrates throughout my body and makes every square inch of me smile. My eyes smile, my heart smiles. I can't be sure, but I think my stomach, my intestines, and even my spleen are smiling. God is laughing, I am smiling, and the time seems right to ask, "Can we make a deal?"

The laughter stops abruptly. "Do I look like Monty Hall to you?"

"No. You look like an acid trip I took in 1969."

Did you ever have one of those moments when you think something so intensely that you're not sure if you just *thought* it or if you actually came out and *said* it? I'm suddenly having one of those moments. Had I just said, out loud, that God resembled a drug hallucination? Apparently, the answer is "yes, I did." I duck, wait for the lightning, and mumble, "I am such an asshole!" Oops. Did I just say *that*? I look around for a hole to jump into but don't find one. Heaven may be holy, but as far as I can tell, it's also "hole-less."

I hear the unmistakable sound of His laughter. No doubt about it, He is definitely laughing. I'm babbling like a fool, and God is laughing. I make a mental note to consider the possibility that those two activities, my acting like a fool and God laughing, are somehow connected, and then I try again.

"Okay, no deals, but can we talk? I mean, may I ask You some questions?"

"Of course you may," He says graciously. "Is there anything in particular that you would like to ask Me?"

Is there anything in particular I'd like to ask God? "Does the Pope shhhhiiii…" I reach into my mouth and grab my tongue before I can finish asking *that* stupid question.

CHAPTER 3

Why Are There Monkeys?

T hey tell me that I was clinically dead for eight minutes. In your normal eight-minute time span, you can smoke a cigarette, jog a mile, or, if you happen to live in Los Angeles, drive at least three and a half feet on the 405 Freeway.

I have no idea how many questions He will allow me, but when God says He'll give you the answers, the least you can do is ask *the* questions. I close my eyes and try to think. I think back to countless nights spent with friends, pondering life's deepest mysteries. The question most often asked was, "If you could talk to God, what would you say to Him?" What indeed.

It occurs to me that my entire life can easily be summed up with the bumper sticker message **"Question Authority"** (and isn't it lovely to realize that one's life can be summarized in a bumper sticker?) That simple slogan has been my mantra since childhood. No subject, large or small, escaped my scrutiny. At home, I questioned my parents. In school, I questioned my teachers. On the radio, I questioned musicians, politicians, scientists, doctors, lawyers, and even the occasional Indian chief.

In parking lots, I questioned inanimate objects. Each time I saw the **Question Authority** bumper sticker affixed to a car, I whipped out my trusty black marker and, just beneath the words, wrote **WHY?** Why? Well, how better to demonstrate my commitment to the questioning of authority than to question the authoritarian placard that was ordering me to question authority?! (You still with me?)

I spent my life questioning everyone about everything, yet as I stand in the presence of the ultimate Answer Man, the mere thought of asking a question makes my tongue seize up like the rotary engine of a rusty Mazda.

"What would you like to know? Surely, you must have at least one question for Me," the Voice chuckles.

What would I like to know? I want to know everything. I want to know where the wind comes from. I want to know why, when rain begins to fall from a cloud, the cloud doesn't just spill all of its rain in one torrential gush, like a burst water balloon. I want to know who killed JFK. I want to know how dolphins keep from drowning when they sleep. I want to know if He has me confused with someone infinitely more worthy than I. I decide to skip that last question, in case the answer is *yes*, in which case I might find myself standing before that other authority figure—the one with the horns and the bad attitude.

As a warm-up question, I ask if He will allow me to ask anything, anything at all.

"Yes," He says without hesitation.

"Will You actually give me the answers?"

"We'll see."

I suffer an involuntary shiver as I again hear my mother's words flowing from God. I take a deep breath. (Still dead and still breathing. Go figure.) I straighten my shoulders and step right up to the plate. "What do You look like?"

"Would that be your first official question for God?" He asks politely.

"No. My first official question for God would be what are the real words to "*Louie Louie*," but I'll settle for knowing what You look like."

"Are you sure? I'd be happy to tell you the lyrics of "*Louie Louie*.""

The thought of God singing "*Louie Louie*" is too much for this dead girl, so I say that if it's all the same to Him, I'd rather discuss His personal appearance.

"People tend to picture You as a very old white man with long, white hair and a long beard. Is that what You look like?"

"No," He says.

"Well, do You have long, white hair?"

"No."

"Do You have a beard?"

"No."

Hmmm, no long hair, no beard. Okay, one item left. "Are You an elderly white man?"

"No."

I realize that I'm dead, so various body parts may not be functioning properly, but I could swear God just said that He isn't white, which causes the words "God is black?" to fall out of my face, followed by the words, "Louis Farrakhan will have a field day with this piece of news."

"I did not say that I am black," the Voice quickly points out and then adds, "I have no color."

How can that be? Even Johnny and Edgar Winter have some color.

"Color is not an issue in My case," He says.

Now wait one minute here. Not black. Not white. No color. No long hair. No beard. I give up, which is pretty much what I say to Him at that point, hoping that He will materialize in front of me. He must have been reading my mind, because the next thing He says is, "My appearance can be overwhelming, and I would not want to cause you any harm."

Harm? Harm?? "Hey, remember me? I'm dead. Harm is pretty much a moot point, don't you think?"

He laughs. Apparently, my death is a source of some amusement to Him.

"Will You at least tell me if You're a…I mean if You have a…" All I want to know is whether God is male or female. Under normal circumstances, that would be an easy question to pose. Unfortunately, since I am dead, breathing and talking to God, there doesn't seem to be anything particularly *normal* about my circumstances, which explains why, at this point, I'm only opening my mouth to change socks.

"Is God of the male persuasion?" I finally manage to say.

"Why does everyone ask Me that question?"

"You're asking me?" I say in something approximating stupefaction.

"Why not?" He inquires. "Where is it written that I have all the answers?"

"Just a wild guess on my part, but how about *in the Bible*?"

"No, it most certainly is not," He says. Before I can ask Him why not, He tells me. "Would you want that kind of pressure?" He laughs. "You humans—you always take Me so seriously! Lighten up, for My sake!"

God just told me to lighten up. It will take me years of therapy to deal with this. (I wonder if Heaven offers therapy.) I shake my head and attempt to refocus. "So, are You male or female?" Simple question, right? Wrong!

"The truth is, I am neither," says the deep, resonant Voice to which I am almost becoming accustomed. Then, the softest, most gentle, and most undeniably feminine voice I have ever heard says, "And then again, I'm both."

Getting dizzy again. Must sit down.

The thought of God being a hermaphrodite is more than I can stand, so I sit. Oh, to be a fly on the wall when Pat Robertson hears about this!

"I have no hair, no beard, no body," God says. "I am a spiritual being. I have no gender."

"Yes, sir. I mean, yes, ma'am." I'm babbling. "Please tell me what I should call You. God? Lord? Father? Yahweh? Allah?"

"I have been known by all of those names and many more," He says.

"What do You prefer to be called?" I ask.

"Man's name for Me does not define Me. You may call Me whatever you wish to call Me. The name you choose is of no importance to Me."

In other words, the names mankind uses when referring to God are irrelevant to God. In the wake of that mind-boggling revelation, I momentarily forget that I am standing on Heaven's doorstep, trying to figure out an appropriate question to ask God. When I remember where I am, at least seven thousand questions appear in my admittedly boggled brain, so I reach in and grab one. "May I ask You about Evolution?"

"Certainly," He says. "What would you like to know about it?"

Images of Jane Goodall with a family of chimps in the wilds of Africa fill my head. As I understand it, Darwin's *Theory of Evolution* posited that the human race evolved from *monkeys*. For me, that has always raised one obvious question, so being, as I am, the uncontested Queen of Obvious Questions, I say, "If Charles Darwin's theory that monkeys evolved into people is correct, why are there still monkeys? Shouldn't they all have turned into people by now?"

The first thing God does is laugh. The second thing God does is inform me that He had asked Charles Darwin a very similar question. The third thing God does is quote Darwin's response. "His exact words were 'Why do You think I called it a *theory*?'"

He obviously finds Darwin's answer quite amusing, because He's laughing, a lot! I find His laughter a tad confusing and tell Him so. He finds *that* amusing, and continues laughing, and suddenly I'm envisioning the whole of the human race serving as a perpetual Martian Floor Show for the literal Powers That Be. What if humanity's primary function is to provide comic relief? I tell myself to remember to ask things like "*what's the purpose of life*," and then, in an attempt to remove the Martian

Floor Show image from the movie screen of my mind, I shake my head. The image remains. I shrug and press on. "So, Darwin was wrong? There's no truth to his *Theory of Evolution*?"

"I did not say that, did I?"

"Well, no, not exactly, but You seemed to be implying it."

"Was I?"

"Well, weren't You?"

Just as my mental choir begins singing "Will The Circle Be Unbroken," the circle is broken by a loud and insistent "No!"

"Then what's the answer? Did the human race evolve from monkeys....or are we all the children of Adam and Eve, who were created by You, sans monkeys?" With that, I relax, certain in the knowledge that I finally posed one question that requires a direct, unequivocal answer. I should have known better.

"Technically, that's more than one question," says He.

Definitely not the response I'm expecting! "Is there a limit to the number of questions I am allowed to ask?" I ask, fearing that if there is, I might have already exceeded it…and that would be very distressing considering the fact that there are several dozen unasked questions currently hopping around on pogo sticks inside my ever-questioning (though apparently no longer living) brain.

"There is a limit to *all* that is created" He informs me.

Did God just tell me that I owe my existence to Creation and not Evolution? Suddenly my brain wants to ask at least three questions, all at the same time, but I settle for "So, what's my limit? How many questions may I ask?"

"Time will tell," He tells me.

"And you won't?"

"I did not say that," He says yet again.

It occurs to me that if I am going to be granted a limited number of questions, I would be wise to pose questions that really matter. (I'm dead, and I'm making a conscious choice to act wisely. If I'd been wise enough to make that choice while I was alive, I might not now be dead. The irony is not lost on me, but I choose to ignore that realization.) "Okay, one question at a time! Evolution—fact or fiction?"

"Fact, of course," He answers matter-of-factly.

"Of course?" I find His response so startling that I actually interrupt Him. Bizarre, but true. "You say that as if Evolution is a commonly accepted fact. It's not. There is a certain segment of the human race that has been debating it for many years!"

"Humans have a habit of debating all sorts of things" God says, adding "the fact that they debate does not negate the facts they are debating."

I let that roll around in my head—*the fact of debating does not render the subject being debated inherently debatable.* Not actually sure that's precisely what He means, but I rather like the concept, debatable though it may be. Moving right along, I say, "So Darwin's *Theory of Evolution* is not, in fact, a theory but is, in fact, a fact?"

"Most assuredly," He says.

So, adding one plus one, I come up with, "Well, that must mean that the Adam and Eve story of Creation is just a myth." Math never was my strong suit.

"No," He says, "it means no such thing!"

By this time, I have accepted the fact that I am well and truly dead. I've also accepted the fact that being dead does not preclude the possibility of being well and truly confused. "How could both Evolution and Creation be facts? Doesn't the existence of one rather disprove the existence of the other?" I am bound and determined to get this one figured out, and standing, as I am, before the One who has already figured out everything, I figure the odds are pretty much in my favor!

"Why can't both be fact?" He asks.

I really should stop figuring! "You're asking *me*?" I blurt.

"Why not?" He replies gently.

"Well, maybe because I'm me and You're...You. I'm not the one who knows everything!" I say, stating the painfully obvious.

"You know more than you think you do," He assures me.

"I do?"

"Yes, you do!"

"Like what?" I ask, desperately hoping that He'll give me an itemized list. What I receive is definitely not an itemized list.

"Time will tell," He says.

And around and around we go. Getting dizzier by the second. I take a minute (or is it just a second?) to catch my breath, quiet the dozens of questions that are fighting for their place at the head of the line (or the head of my head) and start again. "If I understand You correctly, You're saying that Darwin was basically right except for the part where he referred to Evolution as a *theory*, because Evolution isn't a theory, it's a fact, and the story of Creation is also a fact, *and* Evolution and Creation are not mutually exclusive—the existence of one does not rule out the existence of the other—yes?" (if that sentence were any longer it would be on Death Row)

"Yes."

I suppose there are those who find a simple *yes* or *no* to be quite sufficient. I, however, am not one of those. For me, a monosyllabic *yea* or *nay* is a bland and boring thing when compared to an in-depth description of the whys, wherefores, and whatnots of the whatevers of life. So, I do what I seem always to do…I ask for more. "How can they both be fact? If You created the human race, that must mean that the human race owes its existence to You, not to monkeys…doesn't it?"

"Does it?"

"No fair!" I fairly shout, handing control of my vocal cords to the six-year-old who still lives somewhere deep inside my head. "I asked first!"

He laughs…and laughs…and laughs some more. No doubt about it, He's laughing, and I'm pretty sure I am the cause of His laughter. That realization is both amusing and alarming—those two things not being at all mutually exclusive.

His laughter stops abruptly. "Because it is facts that you seek, I will inform you that the human race did *not* evolve from monkeys."

Aha! "So Darwin was wrong! His *Theory of Evolution* is nonsense?"

"I did not say that," He says.

"You didn't? I thought you did!" I stammer. I stammer, He laughs. And laughs. And laughs.

"Apparently, the ability to misunderstand or misquote Me is a human trait that has yet to abate."

As He chuckles, I struggle to articulate my confusion without sounding like an absolute imbecile. I should have known better. "Please help me understand. I don't want to misunderstand or misquote You. You just said that humans did *not* evolve from monkeys, so doesn't that mean that the *Theory of Evolution* is wrong?"

"The human race did not evolve from monkeys, that is true, but that does *not* mean that Evolution is not a fact of life." I wait for Him to continue. My wait is brief. "The human race did indeed evolve. In fact, all life evolves over time. The error is not in the existence of Evolution, but in where that evolution began!"

I find myself wishing for a notebook and a pen. My memory is a notoriously untrustworthy creature. "Can I have something to write this down with?" I ask.

"There is no need for that," He says. Before I can mention that He doesn't know how feeble my memory is, He says, "I am writing it on your Soul. In time, you will remember."

In time? In time for what? I would have asked, but apparently it isn't time for that.

"The evolution of the human race began not with monkeys but with an ancestor of the creature you refer to as an *ape*. Apes and monkeys are not the same" He informs me. And with that, Zoology 101 is officially in session.

"Does that mean that the story of Adam and Eve is a myth?" I ask.

"Indeed not," He answers. "Evolution and creation are not mutually exclusive. All that evolves was created, and all that was created evolves."

I have no doubt that He thinks that clears everything up, and perhaps it does for someone, but not for this girl. "So, which came first?" (I want to say "the chicken or the egg," but for once in my life—in my death?—I somehow manage to bite my tongue.) Instead, I say, "Did You create the ancestors of the ape first, or did you first create Adam and Eve?" That, I think, is the perfect question. Straight to the heart of the matter and certain to generate a precise response. No room for equivocation. I wait for the perfect answer (again, I should have known better).

"Yes," He says.

I still can't see Him, or Her, or Whomever, but I am certain that I can feel, if not actually see, a smile behind the answer He has just provided. I'm dead, and, apparently, He's having a jolly old time. Doing my best to hide my mounting frustration, I say, "Either/Or questions can't really be answered with a *yes* or a *no*, ya know."

"Can't they?...or can they?" He says just before He begins yet again to laugh, and this time I find myself laughing right along with Him.

The laughter soon ends, and the lesson resumes. "The creatures that first populated your world were created by Me, all of them, but as is true of Evolution, Creation is a process. Created beings evolved, grew, adapted, and changed over time to meet the changing conditions of their environment. Life strives to survive and does what it can to ensure that survival. That is the purpose of Evolution."

"And the creation of Adam and Eve? Where do they fit into this scenario?"

"All life was created by Me, and all that lives evolves. Such is the nature of Creation—but life without change, without growth, eventually ceases."

I nod my (still dead) head to indicate that I understand, which I sorta do. "So, You created *all* life—the birds, the bees, and all that lives and breathes, and one fine morning, a critter that had gone to sleep as a monkey's uncle—excuse me, an *ape's* uncle—woke up as a human man. Is that what You're saying?"

"That would be an extreme oversimplification, but if it helps you to understand then, yes, that is what I am saying."

I let that roll around in my now severely addled brain and find myself unable to keep from restating my earlier question, or at least a slightly modified version of it. "In that case, I have to alter my question," I explain.

"Which question? You have asked several," He reminds me.

"True," say I, "but I'm referring to my Evolution question. If people evolved not from monkeys but from apes, my question is: *why are there still apes*? Shouldn't *they* all have become people by now?"

He's laughing again, and I have no doubt that He's laughing at me. Not *with* me, mind you, but *at* me. I can't explain why I don't find that humiliating, but the fact is, I don't. Not in the least. God is laughing at me, and I find it charming, amusing, delightful. Go figure. Obviously, I'm not well. (Well, actually, I'm not only not well, I'm dead…but I can only deal with so many realizations at a time.)

He interrupts my reverie with, "Evolution is a long journey, and that journey, like most long journeys, is not a straight line. Over time, it twists and turns. Picture one thousand wolves living in different locations—different climates—confronting different obstacles to their continued existence. Over the course of many millennia, the wolf grew, adapted, changed, and eventually your world had wolves and collies and corgis and poodles and thousands of other four-legged canines of various sizes and shapes, and yet the wolf has not vanished."

I'm a dog lover. In fact, given a choice between living with a dog and living with a human, I'd choose the dog, so when our conversation finds itself in the land of the canine, I instantly discover that I have a bone to pick with Him. (Sorry.) "That's not fair!' I bark. (Sorry again.) "Wolves were domesticated by humans, and then through selective, intentional breeding, all kinds of dogs were created. That's not Evolution—that's man-made manipulation," I insist, because, of course, those with the least amount of knowledge are invariably the ones most in need of making themselves heard.

"The Chihuahua owes his existence to My creation of the ancestors of the wolf who, over time, evolved into the ancestors of the dog, who, with the intercession of man, evolved into the dog," He explains methodically.

"So, You're saying that You create. Your creations evolve. Some evolve into slightly different versions of the original, while others evolve into unrecognizable versions of the original, thus the continued existence of apes and the concurrent existence of creatures of ancient ape lineage—yes?"

"Yes, I am saying that very thing."

Another person, a wiser person, would probably change the subject at this point, but a wiser person isn't here, and I am, so I say, "And Adam and Eve?"

"What of them?" He asks.

"Did You create Adam and Eve?"

"Indeed I did."

"So You're saying that Adam was not the product of Evolution?"

"Of course he was."

"How could Adam be both a created being and an evolved being?"

I could be wrong, but I'm pretty sure I hear Him make a sound that bears an uncanny resemblance to the noise my father made when he'd become seriously frustrated by my persistent childish questions.

"Some years ago," He begins in a slow, gentle voice, "nine months before you were born, you were just an embryonic assortment of cells."

Odd—kinda spooky actually. I'm having a

momentary thought of my father, and suddenly The Father is talking about, well, about me as a twinkle in my father's eye, so to speak. I would have called that a Twilight Zone moment, but then again, absolutely everything I am experiencing is something of a Twilight Zone moment—a Twilight Zone moment on steroids.

I nod my head, in part to shake out the Twilight Zone theme song that is suddenly playing between my ears and settle in for what I assume will be a lengthy paternal explanation of the birds and the bees.

He continues, "Less than one year later, you entered the world with two arms, two legs, ten fingers, ten toes, lungs, a heart, and all the rest. A tiny human of very limited physical abilities. As the years passed, the cells that had been created grew, changed, and adapted, and eventually you became a fully functioning human."

"I don't know about the 'fully functioning' part," I offer.

He ignores my comment and continues with His monologue. "In the story of your own life, you can see a microcosm of both Creation and Evolution. It is, of course, vastly oversimplified, but perhaps that is the best way to help you understand. It is not a simple subject to comprehend, but sometimes the best way to teach complicated subjects is to reduce them to their most simple and relatable elements." The simpleton in me thanks Him, and then moves on.

CHAPTER 4

Close Encounters of the
Third Cousin Kind

I f the human race is alone in the universe, then a lot of people have been hallucinating for centuries. However, to believe that humans are the best and brightest beings the Universe has to offer is to ascend to a height of arrogance that even the native New Yorker in me is unable to approach. Then again, until an extraterrestrial craft lands in my living room, I will be hard pressed to accept its existence unless, of course, such existence is attested to by an unimpeachable source.

"Why aren't all humans the same color?" I ask. "If we all came from Adam and Eve, why are we off-white, winter-white, pink, red, yellow, beige, brown, and sixty-three shades of black?"

His reply is short. "Would you believe *Evolution*?"

Silly question. I'm standing at Heaven's front door, holding a conversation with God, and I'm dead. At this point I'll believe pretty much any-thing! "So, we all started out the same color and then evolved into a Rainbow Coalition?" say I.

"Who said that Adam and Eve were the same color?" says He.

Let the games begin...

"Am I to conclude that human life on Earth began in the Garden of Eden with an *interracial* couple?"

As I digest that delicious tidbit, He adds yet another. "Who said the Garden of Eden was on Earth?"

And they're off!

Come to think of it, who *did* say that Eden was on Earth? I go for what I think will be the most likely answer. "The Bible." The way I say it makes it sound equal parts answer and question.

He responds with what is zero part question. "The Bible says that the Garden of Eden was made after the creation of Heaven and Earth, but at no time does it actually say that the Garden was *on* Earth."

Okay—time out! Let me see if I'm getting this straight. The Garden of Eden was not necessarily on planet Earth. If that's true, it means there's a possibility that my great-great-great...etc....etc.... etc....great grandparents were...*aliens*? I close my eyes and envision a pair of happy-go-horny little gray folks holding fingers and skipping gingerly through a lush garden.

Grandparent's Day will never be the same!

If I didn't know better, I'd swear that God is playing with me, and come to think of it, I don't know better, so that may be precisely what He's doing. At least that's what He seems to be doing, because the more we talk, the more He laughs.

"Is it true?" I ask. "Is the human race descended from extraterrestrials?"

"Could be," says He.

Could be? What kind of answer is *could be*?

If I'd been in my right mind, I'm relatively certain that I would have kept my mouth shut at that point, but since I am dead, I probably have no right mind to be in. That probably explains why I say, "Could be? Excuse me, but my uncle could be my aunt." Of course, the instant those words fall from my face, I realize that I have chosen to place precisely the wrong relatives into the metaphor. I rub my eyes, desperately trying to erase the image of my bald, eighty-two-year-old, four-foot-nine-inch uncle dressed in the miniskirt and pushup bra of my seventy-nine-year-old, four-foot-seven-inch aunt. Rather than fading, the picture is gaining clarity. I'm getting nauseous. "*Could be* really isn't much of an answer, and You said You would answer my questions," I whine.

"No," He corrects. "I said that you could ask questions. When you asked if I would answer them, what I said was *we'll see*, remember?"

At the sound of those words, I feel another involuntary shiver run down my spine. Okay, so He isn't going to give me answers to all my questions. "Why won't You answer *all* my questions?" I ask.

"Why do so many of your questions begin with the word *why*?" He asks in return.

Excellent question! Why did I always ask *why*? What difference does it make *why* things happen? What really matters is that they happened. The *why* of it really isn't any of my business. "Okay," I admit, "maybe I don't need to know the *why* of things, but that doesn't stop me from being curious." He wants to know what I am curious about—what *whys* did I want to know. I consider a long list of questions that begin with the word *why* and choose to begin with one that is painfully close to my heart.

"Why do people act self-destructively? Why do we do things we know will cause us harm?"

His answer is short and simple. "I don't know."

Stop the presses! Alert the media! God just said "*I don't know*," which begs the question "Huh?" but I opt for a question with a tad more dignity. "How is it possible for God not to know something?" Nothing could have prepared me for His answer.

"I can tell you *what* has happened," He explains. "I can tell you what *will* happen—I won't, however—

but when the subject is the human mind, the *why* is often puzzling, even to Me."

Feeling dizzy. Head beginning to swim.

God just informed me that He doesn't know why we do the stupid things we do any more than we do. So, the next time someone approaches you and says, "Tell me (fill in your name), exactly why did you (fill in your own stupid thing)," you won't get off the hook by saying "God only knows," because, as it turns out, He doesn't. Put *that* on your scalp and scratch it!

CHAPTER 5

⎯⎯∞⎯⎯

I'll Take Gibberish for $800, Alex

P eople who make it their business to con-
vince me that they know their business
have always told me that God knows the
heart of man. Well, okay, if He knows what's
going on in our hearts, He must know why we're
doing whatever it is that we're doing. Doesn't He?
Apparently not.

I listen as His words fill every cell of my being.
"Knowing a man's heart does not necessarily help
you to know his mind. The heart seeks harmony.
The mind often prefers discord".

He gets a quick *Amen* from me on that one. I
have always thought of man's mind as being rather
like Bakersfield, California—not terribly attractive
and a place I'd go only if absolutely necessary. "Why
don't You do something about it?" I ask Him. It
seems like a perfectly reasonable question. I mean,
He is God after all.

"What would you have Me do—make people be less like people?" I may be dead, but I know a rhetorical question when I hear one. He continues, "When I created the human race, I didn't want a species of mindless automatons. I wanted beings who could think for themselves, so I gave you the freedom to choose your actions. With that freedom comes the potential for good as well as for bad."

I almost say "be careful what You ask for—You may just get it!" but instead I say "If You were to start over, would You do things any differently?" I think He is thinking about it, but then, so am I.

I've always wished that artichoke hearts weren't so hard to get to. Maybe He could make them be on the outside. As I'm making a mental picture of a new strain of artichoke whose heart is delicately perched atop the leaves, I hear Him say, "I must admit that the human urge to mate has caused considerable problems over the years."

Excuse me? Where did *that* come from? I'm thinking vegetables, and God's thinking, well...not vegetables. "The urge to *mate?*" I say.

"Yes. The relationship between men and women. It has caused a great many difficulties. Why is that?" I may be dead, but, apparently, I'm not deaf—I just heard God ask *me* a question! Now what do I do?

The perpetual war between the male and female of the human species has always been a favorite topic of mine, and while I am certain that men and women don't get along very well, I'm not at all certain that the reason is directly linked to a fondness for fondling.

"Lots of things separate us, but the primary reason why men and women don't get along is because we speak two entirely different languages," I explain.

"The human race speaks many more than two languages," He reminds me.

Okay, I can see that I am going to have to be more specific. I'm going to have to explain that the language of men and the language of women are entirely different languages. He wants examples. I give Him three.

"A man and a woman go out on a date. He brings her home, and she says *Goodnight* by which she means, *Goodnight*. The man says *Goodnight* but he means *Can I come in?* Then the woman says *I had a lovely time, thank you* and by that she means *I had a lovely time, thank you.* He says *I had a lovely time, thank you,* but he means *I just spent $150 on dinner. Are you sure I can't come in?* Finally, the woman says *I'll call you,* meaning *I'll pick up the phone and dial your number.* When the man says *I'll call you* he means either *goodnight* or *goodbye.*

God laughs. I smile. Making God laugh is a trip.

CHAPTER 6

Take Two Troglodytes and Call Me in the Morning

Gather any group of people and ask the question "Does God exist?" and you will inevitably hear "God must not exist, because if He did, the world would not be so full of evil." For those who would like to believe in the existence of a Supreme Being, this age-old dilemma has been an insurmountable stumbling block.

Rather than tiptoe around the issue, I decide to jump in with both feet. "Why is there so much evil in the world?" I begin with my first foot. "It's one of the main reasons why people have a difficult time accepting Your existence," I add, inserting foot number two.

"People find it difficult to believe in Me because bad things happen? Do they find it difficult to believe in the Devil because *good* things happen?"

He has me there, and I tell Him so.

"The existence of evil in no way invalidates the existence of good," He says, adding, "In fact, the good in man gains strength in the face of evil."

I give that a bit of thought but can't help pointing out that while good may be gaining strength, evil is busy bench pressing half of humanity!

"Would you rather that I interfere in human events?"

Hmmm—would I rather that God made Hitler's mother have a miscarriage? Well, of course I would. Wouldn't you? I would have told Him so, but He has other plans.

"I made a promise to man that I would reserve My judgment of him until a later date. Until that time, he is free to act as he will."

Okay, we're getting to the heart of the matter here. "You have the power to stop an evil man from committing an evil act, so…" That's as far as I get.

"In so doing," He points out, "I would be denying that man the opportunity to redeem himself—to see the evil in his ways and to repent. Would that be the act of a merciful God?"

"It would certainly be merciful to those who were about to suffer at his hand," I say quickly.

His response is quicker. "Suffering is not an entirely bad thing. When you suffer, you gain something."

I can't help myself. I immediately think of all the mothers in the world who, as the direct result of suffering though labor, gain not only children but also a certain body part that can suddenly accommodate two Buicks and a bicycle. I choose not to mention that particular observation, but I do ask Him why life has to be so hard.

"Would you learn to reach if all that you desired was placed into your hands?" He asks me. "Would you learn to jump if there were no obstacles? Would you ever master all the gifts that you possess—all the strengths—all the talents, if, in the course of your life, you were never pushed into exercising them?" Sounds like a purely rhetorical question to me, so I let it slide right on by, and I'm glad I do, because He keeps right on going. "Name just one thing—one relationship, one lesson—that you value, that you acquired without *any* effort."

One thing I got without *any* effort. I got the Mumps with no effort whatsoever, but I'm guessing that isn't what He has in mind. So, okay, one thing I *value*, that I got by doing nothing. Well, off the top of my head...I got...nuthin', so I change the subject. I ask Him why people have the charming tendency to hurt, maim, or mutilate one another.

He is silent for a moment, and when He finally speaks, He sounds as if He is close to tears. "Men kill for love as readily as for hate, for pleasure as well as for pain, out of madness and out of mercy, for sport and for profit. In man, there is no emotion that cannot spark violence." I was about to ask

Him why so many violent acts had been committed in His name, but before I can begin, He offers the answer. "Violent acts have been committed for countless reasons, for no reason at all, and in many names."

I find myself nodding in agreement until, all of a sudden, I'm not nodding anymore—I'm shaking my head and thinking about that '*in the name of God*' Mantra, so, of course, out of my mouth comes what I think is a mathematical certainty: "I'm sure that if we added it all up, You would be the big winner! I mean consider the Spanish Inquisition and the Crusades, and let us not forget..."

Forget about it. He doesn't much care for my math, because He quickly points out, "I don't consider that *winning*. Would you hold Me responsible for every sword-wielding Barbarian who ever shouted Hallelujah just before he hacked off someone's head?" I'm gonna assume that's a rhetorical question, which is good because it *was* a rhetorical question and He isn't done. "When one man kills another, am I to blame?" He asks. Rhetorical again? Not sure, so I say nothing.

It gets very quiet. I say nothing. He says nothing. My silence is followed by His silence, and His silence I can *feel* in every cell of my body. Maybe that wasn't a rhetorical question, after all. "You talking to *me*?" I finally ask.

"Do you see anyone else?" I'm such a dolt I'm actually looking around while He's answering His own question. "The human race is notorious for putting the blame everywhere *except* where it truly belongs. I neither control nor manipulate man's activities. Man, and man alone, is responsible for his actions. He acts as he chooses, and he will be judged accordingly".

I feel the ice thinning beneath my feet as I ask for clarification. "Are You telling me that *everything* the human race has been through happened because *we* made it happen?"

"With the exception of natural occurrences such as earthquakes and erupting volcanoes, yes," He says. "All that man has experienced throughout his history was brought about by his actions or because, rather than making something happen by his action, he permitted it to happen by his inaction."

And just like that, I discover that we humans live in the icy waters of *Lake Damned If We Do, Damned If We Don't*.

"You are responsible for your own life, and in your life, you make choices," He tells me. "Some choices lead you to act, while others lead you to refrain from action."

What about being my brother's keeper? (Nobody in their right mind would want to keep *my* brother!) "Are we responsible for what *we* do, what we don't do, and what the other guy does or doesn't do?" I ask, hoping that the answer will be "no, not if the other guy is a horse's rear end," but I have a nagging feeling that probably will not be God's answer.

"While you haven't the power to control the actions of others, you do have the power to influence those with whom you come in contact." (Don't look now, but this lake isn't just cold—it's deep!) "In the end, a man will do precisely as he wishes, but if you make no attempt to persuade him to do the right thing rather than the wrong thing—the compassionate thing rather than the cruel thing— then you are not blameless when the evil act is committed. By your failure to act, you share in the responsibility for the unrighteous action."

To make absolutely certain that I have gotten the point, He paints a picture that even Stevie Wonder would be able to see. "If a drunken man gets behind the wheel of a car, and you make no attempt to stop him, when he crashes into a school bus loaded with children, you would not need Me to tell you that you are partially to blame, would you?" Ah, the lilting sound of the rhetorical question. "The scope of a man's responsibility is defined by the degree of his morality," He says. The intensity of those words makes my heart ache, and they insist on reverberating in my head, but He isn't finished. "The more moral a man is, the more extensive he perceives his responsibility to be."

I think I see an opening, so I put my foot in it. I suggest that, by that definition, since God is the most moral of all beings, He should bear the most responsibility. I put my foot in it all right. I can feel my toenails tickling my vocal chords as He continues.

"I am responsible for all that I do, all that I have done, and all that I will do. However, if you are implying that I am responsible for all that the human race has done, you are mistaken. It is man, and man alone, who is responsible for the things that he has done and the things he has failed to do. Do you understand?"

It's a question that doesn't really require a response, but with one foot already firmly lodged in my throat, I decide to stick the other one in, if only for the sake of symmetry. "If I'm understanding You correctly, what You're saying is: I'm a Bozo, but not because my mother and my father were certified (not to mention *certifiable*) Bozos. Yes?"

God chuckles. He actually chuckles and, as He does, I find myself wondering what the world's Freudian Therapists will do when they hear about this.

CHAPTER 7

⌒⌒⌒

Christians, Muslims, and Jews, Oh My!

J esus, Allah, and Yahweh—seems everybody is
on a first-name basis with God. You'd think that
with all these religiously-minded people running around, we'd be able to coexist in peace, yet
the battle rages, and the war cry persists. *"My way
or the highway"*—but which way is *His* way? Is there
only one way, and if so, which way is it?

There are Christians, and Muslims, and Bud-
dhists, and Jews. There are cow worshippers, and
tree worshippers, and witch worshippers, but which
worshippers are right? Is there only one true religion, and if there is, what is it? That's what I want
to know, so that's what I ask, and He answers, "I am."
That, of course, inspires me to ask which religion He is, and He tells me, "I am no religion." Okay,
but wait—there's more. When asked to discuss the
difference between Christians, Jews, and Hindus,
for example, He says that all men are equal in His

eyes and the labels they choose to place upon their beliefs are meaningless to Him. In other words, God is the one true religion, but He is no religion, and a man's religion has nothing whatever to do with God's relationship with that man. This will come as quite a shock to a few billion people!

"Religion is a man-made concept," He explains. "It is a collection of rites and rituals, dogmas and edicts, all invented by men in an attempt to control other men. It has nothing whatever to do with Me."

I know I hear it, but I want to be absolutely certain that I understand it correctly, so I ask Him, "Did You just say that religion has nothing to do with God?"

"Yes, that is precisely what I said, and that is precisely what I meant."

Head spinning. Feeling faint. Must sit down.

I sit on my heels, put my elbows on my knees, cradle my face in my hands, and try to absorb what He seems to be telling me. I fail miserably, so I do what I tend to do when I don't know what to do—I open my mouth. "Are You saying that when someone calls out to Yahweh, and someone else calls out to Jesus, and another person calls upon Allah, YOU are the one who takes the call, so to speak?"

"Indeed, I am," He insists.

"You hear *everyone's* prayers?" I ask.

"I do," He answers without missing a beat.

"Regardless of who they are addressing their prayers to?"

He seems to pause. I could assume that His momentary hesitation is the result of His frustration with my inability to wrap my head around His words, but I choose to assume that He isn't frustrated or annoyed with me but is, in fact, taking a moment to gently craft a response that a simpleton such as I will be able to understand.

"Whether a prayer is directed at a tree, a sunrise, or a statue, all prayers are heard," He explains.

"By You?" I ask.

"By Me," He answers.

"Only by You?" I add, to be absolutely certain that I understand what He's saying.

"By Me...and the occasional government agency."

"Not funny!"

"No, I agree, not funny."

Okay, that seems simple enough, but me being me, simple can always be at least a tad more simple, so I say, "In other words, people who practice different religions, no matter what religion that might be, when they pray, they are, in fact, praying to You. Yes?"

"Yes."

"And there's only one You?"

"Only one Me."

At this point, my head feels as if it is spinning like a 45 RPM record, which of course means that

I start to babble, because, well, that's what I do when I'm confused. "You're saying that every prayer that's prayed is prayed to You, whether that pray-ER knows it or not, and regardless of whether that praying person is a Christian, or a Jew, or a Muslim, or a Hindu, or a Jehovah's Witness, or a Mormon, or a…Druid? What about Druids?"

"Druids as well," He says with a distinct chuckle. "Although they seem to have left the building." With that, He emits what can only be called a deep and prolonged belly laugh. (He has no body, thus no belly, but, apparently, that doesn't prevent him from having a hearty belly laugh.)

"Laughing at one's own jokes is frowned upon," I feel obliged to inform Him.

"Not by Me it isn't," He informs me, between bursts of laughter.

I wait for His joyous laughter to subside. He does seem to enjoy it immensely.

Eventually I attempt to summarize all that He just told me about prayer. "So, You're saying that no matter who people address their prayers to—their ancestors, their patron saints, their fairy godmothers—they are in fact praying to You. Yes?"

"Yes. Whether they know it or not, they are praying to Me."

"That's because…" I say, inviting Him to put the icing on the cake.

"Because there is only Me."

There it is, and as precise an answer as it is, it still leaves me with questions, so I ask them. "Muslims hate Jews," I begin, "but…"

"They didn't always," He interrupts.

"Who didn't always what?"

"Muslims didn't always hate Jews," He informs me.

"They didn't?"

"Indeed, they did not," He explains ever so gently. "For a very long time, Muslims and Jews cherished their brotherhood—their shared ancestry. Abraham was, after all, the father of both."

Having grown up in a world rife with headlines decrying Middle East madness and bloodshed, I am astonished by the news that such insanity was not ever so. "Are You telling me that there was a time when the followers of Yahweh and the followers of Allah were not at each other's throats?"

"Indeed I am!"

"Why did that change?" I ask, truly anxious to learn this lesson.

"Because they forgot their kinship, and it saddens Me deeply."

He stops, and suddenly the space that had been occupied by His Voice is occupied by a silence that is not merely deafening, it is drenched in sorrow. I can't be certain, because I can't actually see Him, but I swear it feels like He is crying, and the pain He's feeling floods into every cell in my body. In that moment, I feel a sadness more profound than any I have ever experienced, and suddenly I realize that I am crying. In fact, I'm sobbing uncontrollably. It feels as if the air I am breathing is made of agony.

As I gasp for breath, He interrupts. "You need not cry, My child. This is My sorrow, not yours," He says softly.

"How can I not? I made God cry!" I sob, wiping the back of my hand across my dripping nose.

"No," He says abruptly, "this time it is not you who caused My sorrow."

I snap to attention, dripping nose forgotten, and say, "*I* have made You cry? When?" I ask because His statement seems to require it, but I cringe at the thought that He will provide an answer.

"There have been a number of times, actually," He offers.

I've come this far, so I force myself to continue "Like…when?"

"The first time was when you turned your back on Me."

"I never…" I start and then stop. "Oh, right—when I decided that You didn't exist because of the pony thing. That made You cry?" My knees are buckling, my eyes are filling with tears, and my nose is running all over my face.

"Of course it did. How could it not? When a father loves a child and one day that child decides that she has no father—that is a most sorrowful moment for a father. Is that difficult to understand?"

"No," I answer quickly.

"What else would you like to know? Perhaps the other times that you made Me unhappy?"

I am still wiping my nose as I say, "Uh, no, I think I can guess what they are" (and I'm quite certain that I can).

"Yes, I believe you can," He says softly, adding, "Is there more you would like to ask Me?"

I take a few deep breaths (still dead, still breathing--still mind boggling) and try to collect my thoughts. A few moments pass, or is it just a heartbeat? Time in Heaven bears no resemblance to time on terra firma. In fact, in Heaven, time seems not to exist at all.

He gives me a minute to collect my thoughts, and then says, "All right, have you any more questions to ask?"

I think it is time (speaking of time), in fact well past time, to begin at the beginning—to be orderly about this Question and Answer Session I'm having with God, so I ask Him where He came from. He informs me that He did not come from any place. God did not come from any place. I let that one roll around in my head for a moment or two. It occurs to me that what does not come from any place must, by process of elimination, come from no place.

I tend to think out loud, or at least that's what I tell people. It's more likely that I lack the internal *Editor Gene*. As a result, that which appears in my brain quickly falls from my face completely unedited. This particular personality trait (character flaw?) has no upside that I have ever been able to detect, but its downside is glaringly apparent. I say dumb things on a regular basis. The point I'm making here is that the instant the concept of *no place* arrives in my brain, the following sentence flies from my lips. "God comes from *nowhere?*" Yes indeed, the Queen of Stupid Questions is still in the house.

"Nothing comes from nowhere," He says, "and that which comes from somewhere has a beginning. I have no beginning, for I have always been." I think that means that there was never a time when there was nothing, because there was always something—God.

"So," I offer, "if there was never a time when there was nothing, then there was never a *Big Bang*, because, according to the *Big Bang Theory*, once upon a time (I think it was a Tuesday), a whole bunch of nothing suddenly exploded, right there in the middle of nowhere, and created a whole bunch of something that then traveled to a whole bunch of somewheres. Yes?"

"The universe did not make itself," God says, adding, with a chuckle, "and I find the name *Big Bang* amusing." Apparently, He finds it *extremely* amusing, because He repeats it three more times, laughing harder with each utterance.

CHAPTER 8

───◦◦◦───

Faith, Dope, and Clarity or Three Million Men Named Jesus

O nce upon a time, there was a little girl named Faith. Faith had several things: a blazing fast ball, a blistering tennis backhand, and a brutal childhood. What Faith did *not* have was *faith*. She wasn't alone in this department, but the fact that what she lacked was precisely the thing for which she had been named was an irony that escaped no one's attention, least of all hers.

By the age of eighteen, still not having acquired even a small sample of faith, Faith did the only thing she could think to do—she changed her name. The fact that she found faith not long after giving up both her name, Faith, and her quest for faith, was an irony that also escaped no one's attention, least of all hers.

Juan, Julio, Jorge—all pretty casual, comfortable, easy-to-wear names for a young Latino, but Jesus? Now there's a name a boy really has to work to live up to. "Does it bother You that so many people have named their sons Jesus?" I ask.

"Not at all," He answers. "I consider it a compliment. Imitation is known as the highest form of flattery, is it not? In this case, I see it is an indication of faith."

Ah, faith. What exactly is faith anyway, and how does one go about getting it, I wonder, which, of course, means that that's exactly what I say. (Appears in brain equals falls from lips, remember?)

"Faith is the belief in things not seen, and one has faith the instant that one decides to have it," He explains.

In other words, having faith is just a matter of *deciding* to have faith. Well, that certainly sounds easy. If faith is a belief in things not seen, and God is one of those unseen things, in order to believe in God's existence, all one has to do is make a conscious decision to have faith in God's existence. "I see" I say, not at all certain that I see. That dizzy feeling is creeping up on me again.

Sensing my uncertainty, He adds "One need not be certain that I exist in order to discover that I exist. Many have come to Me while unconvinced of My existence."

The Paradox Alert bell that lives somewhere between my ears begins to clang. "How does someone come to You if they're not even convinced that there is a You to come to? I mean, how would one know where to go if one didn't even know what one was looking for…ya know?" (Going *Valley Girl*—call for backup.)

"One need not *go* anywhere. All you need to do is be still. I will do the rest." He pauses for a moment, and then He tells me the story of a young woman who had no idea what she believed in, or even if she believed in *anything*. She thought she had it all, until the night she looked at everything she had and realized that something important was missing, but she had no idea what that something was.

According to the story, the woman began to cry, and then she began to do something she hadn't done since she was a little girl—she prayed, which seemed like a very odd thing for a nonbeliever to be doing, but that's what she did.

When He got to that point in the story, I had to stop Him and ask a question. "How does someone who doesn't believe in You, pray to You?"

Rather than answering my question in the generic, He answers it by telling me exactly what the woman said in her prayer. "I don't even know if You exist. All I know is that I've been calling all the shots in my life, and all I've succeeded in doing is failing. I have the Midas Touch—everything I put my hands on turns to mufflers. If You do exist, please take over for me. You couldn't possibly do any worse a job than I've done." That's what He says she prayed, word for word, but that's not where the story ends.

By noon of the next day, the woman realized that she hadn't uttered a profane word since she woke up, and for her that was an absolute impossibility. The only time this lady didn't cuss was when she didn't speak. She had tried to clean up her vocabulary on numerous occasions but had never succeeded, yet here she was, six hours into her day, and not one single obscene, crude, or vulgar word had passed her lips. She was so amazed that she said out loud, "Holy shhhh…"

That was as far as she was able to get. That was all that would come out of her mouth. She tried to finish the word, but no matter how hard she tried, the word would not come. She knew she couldn't take credit for her sudden inability to swear like a drunken sailor. After all, she'd tried, and failed, too many times in the past. No doubt about it, something else was going on. It felt to her as if an Angel was grabbing her tongue, and as soon as *that* thought crossed her mind, she knew that her prayer of the night before had been answered. And so it was, and her life was never quite the same again.

When He finishes telling me that story, I find myself wondering what not swearing has to do with an introduction to God, so that's what I ask Him. He says that what she asked in her prayer was that He come into her life, so that's what He did. "I introduced myself to her by bringing about an immediate and obvious change in her—a change she could not fail to notice and for which she could not take credit." From that I conclude that it is possible to begin a relationship with God without first believing in God, and from that I conclude that these conclusions are making me dizzy.

I sit down just in time to hear Him conclude His story with the words "and I've been in her life ever since." For me, that raises another question. Exactly what does it mean to have God in your life? If you have God in your life, is your life trouble free? Inquiring minds (like mine) want to know, so I ask, and He answers.

"Human life is filled with difficulties, but those who trust in Me know that they need not shoulder those difficulties on their own."

That covers believers, but what about nonbelievers? Where do they fit into this picture? "What about Atheists?" I ask. "Where do those who don't believe in You fit it?"

"I cannot take credit for this answer, but I very much agree with it," He says. "I don't believe in Atheists." He begins to laugh with such abandon that whatever I am standing on begins to roll and sway in time to His laughter.

CHAPTER 9

⌒⌒⌒

Kiss My Ass or Miracles, Mets, and Mules

odern history is filled with stories of Miracle sightings—everything from pictures of the Virgin Mary on potato chips to statues crying real tears. In Biblical times, however, Miracles seemed more miraculous, what with stories involving the parting of a large body of water and the raising of the dead. Can any of these stories, modern or ancient, be believed?

What with all the laughing He's doing, it feels like God is actually enjoying my company. That in and of itself seems miraculous to me, so it seems like the perfect time to bring up the subject of Miracles. He asks me to be more specific. Am I looking for the definition of a Miracle or an example of a Miracle? Considering the venue, I choose both.

"By definition," He explains, "a Miracle is something that can happen only if I make it happen."

Okay, definition of the word Miracle, covered, but now the real deal—an *example* of a Miracle. Just for fun, I request a Miracle that occurred during my lifetime, if one had occurred during my lifetime.

"Miracles happen every day," He says.

"They do?"

"Of course they do. The birth of a child is a Miracle," He says.

"It is? I thought childbirth was a natural process. A sperm meets an egg, and presto, nine months later, a baby is born. It just happens," I say.

"Nothing just happens by itself," He reminds me. "Have you never wondered how it is that millions of different cells can combine in just the right way and in just the right amounts? How something as basic as an egg can become something as complex as a human? Does that not seem miraculous to you?"

"Yes, of course it does," I say, "but I thought You said that a Miracle was something that happened only if You made it happen. Are you saying that babies are born only because You make them be born?"

"I created the means by which all that is, is. I created the cells that produce babies, and I gave those cells to the human race. In a sense, it is true that children are born because of Me, but I only gave mankind the tools to enable the birth of a child. It is the human race that creates each child."

As His words wash over me, He adds, "You

would not credit the maker of paint with the creation of Michelangelo's painting on the ceiling of the Sistine Chapel, would you?" I've never been to Italy, but I've seen photographs of the magnificent chapel ceiling. It certainly looks miraculous, and I doubt that anyone would credit the inventors of paint with that miraculous work of art. Suddenly my art appreciation reverie is interrupted.

"Think of a newborn baby as a beautiful loaf of bread," God urges. "I provide the ingredients, but it is the bakers who actually create the bread."

"Humans are the bakers, yes?"

"Yes," He says.

Well, all right. That makes sense to me, but it isn't the type of Miracle I'm looking for. I'm hoping to hear about something bigger. Something more like a burning bush that talks or an ocean that stops being an ocean and turns into a path. He must have been reading my mind again, because out of nowhere, He says, "The New York Mets winning the World Series in 1969 is one of My favorite twentieth-century miracles."

Getting very dizzy. Experiencing major head spinnage. Must sit down.

"Baseball? The Mets winning the World Series? You call *that* a Miracle?" I babble.

"Considering their record, wouldn't you?" God says through peals of laughter.

Now hold on a minute! The parting of the Red Sea. The Virgin Birth. The Burning Bush. *Those* are Miracles I can almost wrap my head around, but the Mets winning the World Series? "I thought the purpose of Miracles was to prove that You exist," I say.

"It is, in part," He responds. "Are you familiar with the story of the mule and the two-by-four?"

I shake my still-spinning head and prepare to hear the story of the mule and the two-by-four, which goes like this:

Once upon a time, a Quaker was driving his mule-drawn cart down a dirt road when suddenly, the mule stopped and sat down. The Quaker asked the mule to stand up. The mule sat. The Quaker ordered the mule to stand up. The mule sat. The Quaker begged the mule to stand up, and still the mule sat. The Quaker pulled a two-by-four from the back of his cart and cracked it over the mule's head. The mule stood up.

"Why would a Quaker hit a mule over the head with a board?" I blurt.

"Because," says the Lord, "the first thing you must do is get the creature's attention."

I picture the Quaker. I picture the mule. I picture the two-by-four, and then I try to picture the connection to the New York Mets. I fail, so He does it for me.

"On that night in 1969, after the Mets won the

World Series, millions of people were joyously calling out My name and giving thanks. Before that night, more than half of those people had never so much as acknowledged My existence."

"I see," I say, certain that I saw. The Mets were the two-by-four, and a few million New Yorkers were the mules. That sounds about right to me.

CHAPTER 10

───⊙⊙⊙───

People, People Who See Dead People...

I know people who see dead people. I know people who see themselves in long-dead people. I know a man who routinely channels a man who has been dead for over a century. I know a woman who routinely talks to her abusive dead mother who, though dead, is still abusive. I know a couple who believe that they were a couple a couple of centuries ago. I also know that I've been known to consider all of those people to be at least slightly off their rockers for as long as I've known them.

Have you ever wondered what happens to us when we die? (Well, of course you have. Why else would you be reading this book?) Our bodies stop. We all know that, but energy—which is what we're essentially made of—can't be stopped, so where does it go? What happens to all that energy? Is there such a thing as a Soul? What is it? What happens to it when we die? What about ghosts? Do they exist?

Well, one question and one answer at a time.

"Where does our energy go when we die?" I ask.

"It merges with the energy of the universe, like a thread blending into a tapestry," He explains.

"And the Soul? What is that?"

"The Soul is a combination of that energy and Spiritual Essence".

When I ask what *Spiritual Essence* is, He explains that it's a part of Him. In fact, it's the cord (so to speak) that connects us to Him. Combine our energy with that Spiritual Essence and what you get is the Soul, and since our Soul contains a Spiritual Essence that is part of God, there is a part of us that lives forever, because in us is a part of Him, and He lives forever.

"Where does all of that stuff go when our bodies die?" I ask.

He tells me that this life cycle of ours is, in fact, a journey, and when our journey is over, our energy and our Spiritual Essence combine to form a new body, a *Spiritual Body*, in which we can move back and forth through time and space.

"So that's what a ghost is?"

"*Ghost* is a word people apply to images they do not understand," He tells me. "In truth, those who have seen what they refer to as a *ghost* have seen the transformed body of a Spiritual Essence—the ethereal embodiment of a Soul."

If I'm understanding correctly, God just said that we *can* see dead people!

"And no, their purpose is *not* to *haunt* the living." There He goes again, walking around inside my head. That was going to be my next question. "They appear to you because their work is not yet finished. They have a lesson they must teach or a message they must communicate."

"In other words, ghosts are Souls who are doing some unfinished homework. Okay, but what about *haunted houses*?" I ask. "Pictures flying off walls. Doors slamming by themselves. Dishes sailing through the air. What's that—spiritual PMS?"

"There is no PMS in the spiritual body." He chuckles.

At last—a *significant* up-side to being dead! I remind Him of my haunted house question, and He reminds me of His mule and the two-by-four story. Apparently, flying dishes are a spirit's way of getting someone's attention. I make a mental note to switch to paper plates.

CHAPTER 11

—◦◦◦—

Will the Real Marie Antoinette Please Stay Dead

W hy is it that everyone who claims to have lived before says that in a past life they were a Prince, a Queen, or an Indian Chief? I know a woman who claims that she used to be Marie Antoinette. I've never met anyone who said that in a past life they were poor, homeless, or stupid. Why is that?

"Reincarnation? Possible or impossible?" I ask.

"With Me, *nothing* is impossible," He says, emphatically.

Rule number one of the question-and-answer format: Broad questions bring broad answers, this broad suddenly remembers. Time to narrow my focus. I want to know if anyone has ever lived as one person and then come back to life as another person entirely, in another place, at another time. That's what I want to know, so that's what I ask.

"It has been known to happen" He tells me.

"When? Where? Why?" All those words fly out of my mouth and He answers them all.

"When it was appropriate. In various places, and because I chose for it to be so."

"I've often had the feeling that I'm one of those people who has lived before. Have I? I mean, did I?"

"That is one of many things that you will know at the precise time that you *need* to know it," He says.

I assume that means that *now* isn't the time, but if not now, when? "I didn't know when I was alive, and now that I'm dead, You're saying that it *still* isn't time for me to know. Does that mean that there is some other time period that I don't know about?"

"There are many time periods that you do not know about, and that you will not know about, until the time comes for you to know about them."

Getting dizzier. Head spinning.
Shortness of pants.

"Are there reasons for everything that happens?" I say, changing the subject and holding my dizzy head.

"Yes. To believe otherwise is to believe that things happen of their own accord".

That sets my head to thinking, and head thinking is always preferable to head spinning. He's got me thinking that if there are reasons for *everything*, then nothing can happen by mere coincidence, and presto, the moment that thought slides through my cranium, I hear Him say, "Coincidence implies random occurrence. Nothing is random." (Coincidence? I think not.)

I mull this over for a moment and try to wrap my head around the concept that there is a reason for everything, nothing is random, and there is no such thing as coincidence. Okay, that being the case, I'm confused. "If there are reasons for everything, why do so many things seem to happen for no reason whatsoever?" I ask.

His answer is immediate. "The fact that you cannot find a reason for something does not mean that it has no reason. If you cannot find the key to your home, does that mean that your home has no key?"

CHAPTER 12

Of Mice and Menageries

No book has sold more copies, been read by more people, or been debated by more scholars than the Bible. Some say the Good Book is an anchor for the believer that steadfastly roots him to hallowed ground. Others claim it is an anchor for the befuddled that sinks to the depths and prevents them from moving of their own accord. While some would gladly give their lives in its defense, others would, with equal passion, use it for kindling.

I begin with as much subtlety as I can muster. "Some people say that the stories in the Bible are not meant to be taken literally, but need to be interpreted." (Okay, so I'm not very good at mustering subtlety. What else is new?)

It feels as if He has been waiting for this question, because His answer begins immediately. "The Bible was written by men and therefore is not perfect, as nothing done by man can be perfect."

Well, that certainly opens a door for me to walk through, so in I walk. "In other words, there are mistakes in the Bible?"

"Mistakes, misunderstandings, misinterpretations, assumptions—as with everything man does, he puts some of himself into it," He explains.

"So, the Bible is not, in fact, the Word of God?"

"It would be more accurate to refer to the Bible as a *reflection* of My word."

"A reflection?"

"An image," He says, "an image of the original."

I consider that for a moment and then ask, "Well, in that case, how are we to know what's true and what's not when we read it?'"

"By reading it and relying on My guidance to understand My word, rather than relying on your own understanding."

Here I am, standing in His presence and struggling to wrap my head around His words, so the thought of understanding His meaning when I am somewhere other than on His doorstep is rather a bridge too far, as it were, and so I ask, "How are we supposed to do *that*?"

"By *trying* to do that," He says flatly.

"By trying? By just *trying*?" I ask with more volume than is appropriate, considering the setting.

"Yes, by just trying," He says again. "I do not expect My children to know what they are too young to know. Do you?"

"Uh, no," I mumble.

"When My children try to understand Me, or to know Me, I do not expect them to achieve that understanding or knowledge on their own. When My children reach out to Me, I reach out to them, as any loving father would. Do you understand?"

"But the Bible," I blurt, "the Bible is a book that…"

He interrupts, "The Bible is a book that was written by men. I exist within its pages, in *spirit*, just as I exist in all things in spirit. I am there for all to find, and they can, if they seek to embrace not the words but the spirit that inspired the words."

I let those words roll around in my head for a moment or two, and then a few more words fall out of my mouth. "In other words, there are words in the Bible that are *not* Your words?" (I'm like a dog with a bone, and I can't seem to let go of it.)

"The Bible is a *reflection* of My words, and a reflection is not the thing itself, but a vision of the thing. Seek not the reflection. Seek instead the One who is reflected."

I have a sudden feeling that He has said all He intends to say on the subject, but I still have questions, and since He Himself urged me to ask questions, I decide to continue. "Was there a flood?"

"There have been many floods," He says.

"Well, was there an Ark?...and a Noah?"

"Yes," He answers.

Okay, so there was an Ark, and there was a Noah, but how did Noah get all those animals on board? How was he able to tell a male frog from a female frog? Does the female croak in a higher key? The more I think about Noah and his family spending all that time on that boat, with all those animals, the more impossible it seems to me (not to mention odiferous!).

Before I am able to get the question out of my mouth, He presents me with the answer. "The animals entered the Ark because I inspired them to do so."

Here we have yet another case of words in brain falling unimpeded out of my mouth. "You inspired them, and they marched right in. Just like that?"

"Yes, just like that" and *that* is His final word on the subject.

CHAPTER 13

---⊶∞∞⊷---

And Why Were You Born?

You can ask "*why is the sky blue*" or "*how many Angels can dance on the head of a pin*" or "*who wrote The Book of Love*" but no question is more fundamental than "*why are we here?*" Right?

No point beating around the bush (burning or otherwise). "What is the purpose of life?" I ask.

"The purpose of life is to discover the purpose of life," says He.

Well, that clears up everything, doesn't it? "We were born to figure out why we were born?" I stammer.

"Among other things," He chuckles (and yes, He does chuckle!).

Okay, I'll bite. "What other things?"

"To love," He says.

"We were born to figure out why we were born and to love?"

"Certainly. Why? Did you think you were born to shop?" He obviously gets a kick out of that concept, because He laughs long and hard. I decide to assume that that was a rhetorical question.

"I thought You were going to tell me that the purpose of life was slightly more profound than 'we were born to love'."

His laughter stops. "What could be more profound than love? What did you think I would say the purpose was?"

Oh darn—now I have to come up with an answer. Asking questions is my forte. I'm a tad shaky in the answer department. "I don't know. Maybe something like *the purpose of life is to figure out who we are.*"

"Absolutely," He says. "Anything else?"

Wait. Hold on. I thought I was the one asking the questions. "*The purpose of life,*" I offer, "*is for us to discover our connection to You?*"

"Precisely. Very good," He responds.

I seem to be on a roll, so I go for three. "*The purpose of life is for us to figure out what is sacred and to then share it with others.*"

"Indeed it is," He says, sounding pleased with me as He says it, which causes a serious shiver to run up my spine.

As I shiver, I wonder why He didn't say all those things when I first asked Him about the purpose of life (and, of course, what my brain wonders, my mouth wonders). "Why didn't You just tell me all those things?"

"Because if I had told you what the purpose of life was, you wouldn't have discovered it for yourself, and that, after all, is the purpose of life!" He is having fun with me again. I can tell because He laughs and says, "I'm having fun with you."

CHAPTER 14

⬦⬦⬦

My Karma Ran Over My Dogma

Fate, Kismet, Destiny—all words that mean the same thing—*what will be, will be*. But what of *reason*—that thing that separates us from the beasties? Were we not imbued with cognitive powers—with the ability to decide for ourselves and to act according to our own desires? If we are in charge of our own lives, if we are captains of our own ship, how is it possible for Fate to exist? Is our future written before we live it, or do we write it as we live?...and what about Nancy? (Okay, that was a Firesign Theatre reference. Sorry.)

"Is there such a thing as Fate?" I hear myself ask.

"Fate is one of man's most clever inventions," God says. "It is a tool by which he frees himself of responsibility for his actions."

Okay, now we're on to something. Fate is man's Get Out of Jail Free card. ("No, I did not kill your hamster. It was just his time to die.") "If there's no such thing as Fate, then there's no such thing as Destiny, or predestination, or the concept that we're all acting out a script that's already been written. Is that true?" I ask.

"I gave man the gift of Free Will," He reminds me. "What man does is dictated by what man *chooses* to do. At every turn, you are free to choose the road you will travel. I do know which choice you will make before you make it, but that is not the same as predestination, because the choice is entirely up to you."

Well, that's an interesting concept. At any given fork in life's road, we are free to choose whichever path we prefer, but He knows, in advance, which choice we will make. Slide your feet into *those* slippers!

"To summarize," I say aloud, "it isn't written in the stars, or in Your Day Planner, that on such and such a date, such and such a thing is going to happen to such and such a person?" Did I just say that? I'm sounding like a blithering idiot here. Well, that proves my theory—the older I'd grown, the dumber I'd gotten. The progression is now complete—I'm dead, and I've become a total moron!

"With a belief that things happen as they are *destined* to happen, a man may reason that it makes no difference what he does. In fact, what a man does or does not do makes *all* the difference. The whole of man's life is determined by man himself.

His tomorrows are built on the actions he takes today. With each choice he makes, he charts the course of his own life."

"And death?" I ask. "Do we chart the course of our own death, or are we born with only a certain amount of time in our account?"

"Man's passage from the physical to the spiritual plane is an immutable fact of life, and while he can accelerate the arrival of the inevitable, it is not within his power to prevent its eventual occurrence. The primary architect of a man's life—and death—is man himself."

"That must mean that it's not Fate that I'm here right now, right?" Yes indeed, the Queen of the Stupid Question has not left the building!

God begins to laugh, and this time He's not laughing *with* me…he is definitely laughing *at* me! "My question wasn't *that* funny," I insist.

"Yes, it was," He replies. "I give man indications every day that he and he alone writes the story of his life, and yet with at least one finger, he clings tenaciously to the amusing notion that *what will be will be*. The truth is, what *you* make be will be because things don't merely *be* by themselves."

I could be mistaken, but I'm fairly certain that I just heard God speak Ebonics. Whitney Houston, we have a problem!

CHAPTER 15

—◦○◦—

Don't Sin Under the Apple Tree...

There's right, there's wrong, and then there's Sin. In the lexicon of most religious doctrines, it's a category unto itself. But what exactly is Sin? Are there big Sins and little Sins? Many a young Catholic boy has run screaming from Sunday School after being convinced by yet another ruler slap to the knuckles that there was no hope for his redemption—he had committed the Mortal Sin of…(enter your favorite Mortal Sin here). Then there are the Venial Sins, named for the Brothers Venial—makers of marginal Northern California wine. (Kidding—only kidding.)

I begin with the basics. "What is Sin?"

"Sin is a thought or an action that is an affront to that which is sacred," He says.

"Okay, well, what, exactly, do You mean when You say *sacred*?"

"Sacred is holy. Sacred is divine. Sacred is…Me."

"You're saying that a Sin is a thought or an action that is an affront to You?"

"Yes," He replies. Though His answer seems simple, in its simplicity, it covers a lot of ground and leaves me tongue-tied....but only for a moment. "Are all Sins forgivable? Will You forgive us, no matter what we do?"

"All Sins but one may be forgiven," He says flatly. I am about to ask Him to name that one Sin, but He renders my unspoken question moot. "I have given man many indications as to the nature of that one unforgivable deed, but it is up to man to come to terms with that one act and to decide for himself whether or not to commit it. To spell it out for you—to detail the precise nature of that Sin—would be to remove from man the full responsibility for that choice, and that I will not do. I ask very little of man, but what I do ask, I ask without reservation."

From the look of things, I have arrived at my first dead end in God's neighborhood, but being the Queen of both the Stupid and the Obvious Question, I am compelled to say, "You're not going to tell me, are You?"

"You already have all the information you need to discover the answer on your own. I will not do everything for you. If I did, there would be no point to your existence." Well, we wouldn't want that, now would we? (Would we?)

Okay, so there's one thing—just one thing—that we can choose to do, for which we will not be forgiven. However, it is up to us to discover what that one thing is. "What if we can't figure it out?"

"That which man truly cannot do, I do not expect him to do. Unfortunately, man uses the word *cannot* far too often. He employs it to cover that which he does not wish to do, that which he fears to do, and that which he has never before attempted to do. In reality, there are precious few things man cannot do, and discovering the one Sin for which there is no forgiveness is not one of them." No doubt about it—this is a dead end, so I let my mind travel in a new direction.

If God can make a peacock and a rainbow, why would He make a platypus? (I mean really—have you ever looked at a platypus?!) Why are there things like poison ivy and quicksand and cockroaches? Sure, I could ask all those questions, but I don't. Instead, I say, "You created so much beauty and so much that is good and nourishing and healthy for us, but You also created things that are dangerous for us. Why?"

"Even healthy things can be dangerous, if used improperly," He answers.

Aha—I think I see an opening. All ahead warp nine. "What about the things that are unhealthy no matter how you use them? Like heroin. Why would You create something that was nothing but dangerous?" I have Him on this one.

"I did not make heroin," He says.

Uh oh, He's tap dancing. I've got Him for sure. "Okay, so You didn't make heroin, but you did make the flowers that heroin is made from!"

Got Him!

"I also made volcanic lava, but I did not tell you to eat it" He generously points out, adding "I take full responsibility for all that I do. What man does with all that he has been given is his responsibility"

Ooops, don't got Him.

CHAPTER 16

⸺◦◦◦⸺

How Much Is That Pony in the Closet?

As a child of six or seven, I would kneel at my bedside and say my prayers each and every night. *"Now I lay me down to sleep. I pray the Lord my Soul to keep. If I should die before I wake, I pray the Lord my Soul to take...and God, please give me a pony."*

I prayed that exact prayer every night for months, religiously (so to speak), until one morning when, seeing no pony, I concluded that I must not have had God's correct phone number. (It was less painful than concluding that God just didn't like me.) Well, okay, thought I, if I must go through life without my pony, then God will have to carry on without my prayers. That'll teach Him! (As a child of six or seven, I was tough!)

"Do You hear everyone's prayers? Do You see everything we do? Do You watch all of us, all the time, so You know when we're bad and when we're...

really bad?"

"I think you have me confused with Santa Claus." He chuckles.

"Devout believers claim that You are omnipresent—You're everywhere, all the time. Are You?"

"Of course I am. That is My nature," He says matter-of-factly.

A flag goes up in the back of my (dead) head—a mental bookmark. I want to be sure to remember those exact words, because I have a feeling that He is painting a very large picture with the simple phrase "*that is My nature*." Bookmark firmly in place, I press onward. "Okay, so You're everywhere, all the time—but You're not *watching* us all the time?"

"I am aware of everything and everyone, everywhere—I need not *watch*," He says.

As another bookmark plants itself in my brain, I remember my pony. I want to know why I never got my pony! "You see us, but You don't necessarily watch over us, okay, but what about our prayers? Do You hear everyone's prayers?" I ask.

"I do."

"Okay, You *hear* everyone's prayers, but do You *answer* everyone's prayers?" Thanks to the total lack of pony in my childhood, I was certain that I already knew the answer, but the six-year-old in me just had to ask the question.

"People pray for all sorts of things," God begins,

"things they want, things they need, and things they just *think* they need." I'm sure they do, but that doesn't answer my question, and it's a question that's been waiting for an answer since I was a little girl in, if not desperate *need*, at least desperate *want* of a pony. Inquiring minds and pony-starved girls need to know!

Before I can restate my question, He says: "A prayer should not be a shopping list. Would you think it appropriate to call Me on the telephone and say *'Hello, God, today I'd like a new car, a diamond ring, and a vacation on the French Riviera'?*"

I'm thinking that's a rhetorical question, but, rhetorical or not, I feel compelled to respond with "Oh no, not me. Never! I wouldn't do that" and various other noises of a sucking-up nature.

"You would be surprised by the sheer number of people who think that *that* is absolutely appropriate," He says with a decidedly disappointed tone in His voice. "Many people seem to think that I exist for the primary purpose of granting wishes. I am not a Genie!"

"No, of course You're not a Genie. I never thought of You as a Genie, but if You hear all prayers, and You *answer* all prayers, then...why didn't I get my pony?" Okay, I admit it. After all these years, I'm still peeved about the pony thing.

"Ah yes, your pony."

"You heard me asking for a pony?"

"Of course I did," He says, gently.

"So, You heard my prayers, and yet, no pony. May I ask why?"

"An answer to a prayer is not the same as the granting of a wish".

I want to make sure He knows that I'm paying attention so I say "I know, You're *not* a Genie!"

"Indeed, I am not! All too often, when people come to Me in prayer, they ask for something that they think they need. What people *think* they need is not always what they truly need. If what is best for them is to not have that which they have requested, I answer their prayer by not giving them what they asked for."

Translation: *sometimes the answer to a prayer will feel like a prayer unanswered.*

I picture the pony standing in my closet between my cheerleader Pom Poms and my rabbit fur miniskirt, and I forgive God for not giving me that horse. The silly critter probably would have eaten my Pom Poms and pooped on my rabbit fur miniskirt!

CHAPTER 17

⌘

If He's Ugly, Stupid, and Rude, He's Probably Not the Devil

He has horns, a long tail, and a pitchfork. Well, at least that's what the Devil looks like on Halloween, but then again, I thought God was an old white guy with a beard, so what do I know?

As the story goes, once upon a time, God created a drop-dead gorgeous, smart and talented Angel whom He named Lucifer. One day, Lucifer checked himself out in the mirror and decided that *he* was the slickest dude in town and that he—not God—should be running Heaven. He rounded up a bunch of disgruntled Angels and staged a coup. The coup failed, and Lucifer and his gang of cherub chumps were promptly evicted from Heaven. At least that's the story told to little boys and girls in Sunday School (or, as in my case, Saturday School).

"Yes, the Devil does exist," God says casually. "As for what he looks like—he is one of My very best creations, so what do you think he looks like?"

Is this a trick question? Okay, so my assignment is to envision the best-looking male humanoid who ever lived, and I'm kinda sure that, dead or alive, I can do that. I picture the most beautiful man I've ever laid…eyes…on. Oh my, what a lovely picture! The mental image I'm conjuring up is absolutely delicious, but suddenly I remember where I am and poof—lovely mental image, all gone. Sigh. What did I learn from this? I learned that, on the basis of looks alone, if I met the Devil in a dark alley, I'd be in no particular hurry to leave that alley.

Okay, so the Devil actually exists, but what does he want? Well, according to He who knows all, what the Devil wants is *revenge*. He was, after all, evicted from what can only be considered the most magnificent house ever built. So, what we have here is a really smart, really handsome, really cheesed-off guy who's looking for a rematch. He's been in training for quite a while, and all that's left for him to do now is recruit a few more players for his team—pick up a few free agents, and fill out his bench. And how does he get people to play for his team? How does the Devil go about getting what *he* wants from people? Simple—he gets it the old-fashioned way—by giving people what *they* want.

Attention shoppers: Today on aisle 666, the most gorgeous man who ever lived will happily grant your every wish. (And isn't that just what we need—another gorgeous, gift-giving man who is nothing but bad for us?!)

CHAPTER 18

A Rabbi, a Priest, and a Monk Walk into A...

I grew up in small-town Americana of the 1950's. Like many tiny towns of that bygone era, it was home to one barber shop, one drug store, one traffic light, two bars, one whore house, and, perhaps for the sake of spiritual symmetry, one convent and Catholic school. Maria Regina School for Girls accommodated the usual suspects—old nuns, young girls, and one future porn star. (More about the latter later.)

I smoked my first cigarette in the dense woods that surrounded the convent. Those woods saw many firsts. (Insert your adolescent imagination here. We certainly did.) As I inhaled my third puff of my first cigarette (a Tareyton, if memory serves), a black-clad creature of vague proportions stepped out from behind a tree. Her shrouded body and blindingly white complexion were enough to cause me to choke on my cigarette and run screaming from the woods.

I wish I could say that as a result of that experience I never smoked another cigarette, but alas, I cannot say that. I can, however, report that from that day to this, I have had a pathological fear of forest-dwelling, habited nuns.

Yes, I know, you want the porn star story. This is a book about my meeting with God, and you want a story about a world-famous porn queen? Well, okay, if you insist.

Maria Regina School for Girls—a stoic enclave of Catholic chastity—became the subject of global fascination when it was discovered that the school's alumnae list of aspiring Vestal Virgins included none other than that international star of stage, screen, and salacious mind, Linda Lovelace, the original *Deep Throat*. There you have it. (I didn't say it would be a long story.) Now go say sixteen Hail Marys and gargle.

"How does one get into Heaven?" I ask God.

"With My blessing," He tells me.

I am sure that I'm not at all sure what He means by that. "We receive Your blessing based on...what? How well we succeed in business? How many charities we support? How kind we are to the homeless?"

"Actions will not guarantee anyone access to Heaven," God tells me. "Entrance into My Kingdom is based upon one's relationship with Me."

With those words, another bookmark lands in my head. "Are You saying that having a relationship with You is a criterion for entrance into Heaven?"

"I am."

"That means that Atheists need not apply?" I say, more to myself than to Him, but He responds.

"Not necessarily." The bookmarks are piling up inside my addled brain.

"Can a person who has done bad things get into Heaven?"

"If Heaven were reserved for those who had never sinned, it would be a rather empty place," He replies.

There are knuckleheads in Heaven? That could mean that my late father, a card-carrying knucklehead if ever there was one, might be there. With that realization, my mind starts making a mental list of things my dear, departed, knucklehead of a father needs to answer for. The list is long. Much 'splainage is required. Before I let myself envision a confrontation with Daddy Dearest, I want to make absolutely certain that I understand what I've just been told. "In other words, a man can spend his entire life doing hateful, despicable things, but if, with his last breath, he asks for Your forgiveness, the doors of Heaven *will* open for him?"

"It is possible," says the One for whom all things are possible. "All have an equal opportunity to be forgiven for their Sins."

Where's the justice in *that*, I wonder…aloud, unfortunately. "How does one moment of '*I'm sorry, please forgive me*' wash away years of cruel, despicable behavior?"

"That is the very nature of Mercy, and that is My promise to the human race. Forgiveness is available to all who seek it," He says ever so softly.

All who seek it? Regardless of race, creed, color, or…religion? "Do a Catholic, a Jew, and a Muslim have an equal opportunity to get into Heaven?" I ask.

"All have an equal opportunity to enter Heaven," He replies.

Oh, to be a fly on the wall when
the Pope hears this!

CHAPTER 19

---ⲟⲟⲟ---

Tonight on the Late Show—Dead People Cook Dinner

I t seems that long about the time that we figure out who we are and what we're supposed to be doing on Earth, it's time to catch the last bus out of town. We spend a few decades figuring out how to make our various body parts function properly. We spend the next couple of decades figuring out how to make our various body parts function properly with the various body parts of a variety of other people. We spend the *next* couple of decades taking medications to soothe the aching body parts we were playing with all those years. Then we die. Speaking in strictly technical terms, I would have to say, "That sucks!"

I always assumed that I knew the answer to this question, but considering my current circumstances, I think it might be instructive to seek the definitive answer. "What is death—a beginning, or an end?" I ask.

"Consider birth," He begins.

I don't want to consider birth—I want to consider death.

"Consider birth," He repeats. (Okay, if He insists, I'll consider birth). "Is it a beginning or is it an end?"

"It's a beginning," I say, with the kind of absolute certainty displayed only by those who have no idea what they're talking about.

"No, it is *not*," He says, with the kind of absolute certainty displayed only by those who know exactly what they're talking about. "Birth is both a beginning *and* an end. It is the beginning of one life and the end of another. At the moment of birth, the life that had been lived in one world comes to an end, and a new life, in a new world, begins. Such is death—the end of a life in one world and the beginning of a life in another."

Well, that's just fine and dandy, but for those of us who have been left behind, death is the beginning of only one thing—a lot of grief! Death robs the living of contact with those who have died, and that can be agony for those still breathing.

"It need not do that," He insists, reading my mind yet again. "Those who have died have merely passed from the physical to the spiritual plane. Contact continues for those who know how to hear it. Think of it as moving from one place to another. You can still have contact with your departed loved ones. You just have to know their new phone number, so to speak".

"We just have to know their new phone number? Are You telling me that it's possible for the living to communicate with those who have died?"

"Indeed, I am".

My first thought is *there are phones in Heaven?* My second thought is a bit more to the point—*contact with the dead is actually possible?* Am I being told that those talk show-haunting, two-hundred-dollar haircuts on two-dollar heads are speaking the truth when they tell the lady in the third row that her late Granny Flabbyface is standing in the corner, baking turnip tarts?

Suddenly we have head spinnage and a desperate need for 'splainage!

"How, *exactly*, do the living communicate with the dead?"

"With the Soul," He answers.

We can hear with our Soul? I try to picture the part of my Soul that I'd have to press up against the wall in order for it to hear the voices of the departed on the other side. Good thing I'm double-jointed.

"You hear with your Soul by listening with your Soul, and when you listen with your Soul, you silence your mind" He explains.

Silence my mind? Not likely. I've got at least a dozen different people living inside this head of mine—and silence is a virtue that not one of them possesses. Speaking of hearing voices in my head,

I ask, "Do You talk to us?"

"Of course I do," He answers.

Does that mean that the voice in my head that insists that baggy pants make me look as if I'm wearing loaded diapers, is actually the voice of God? Oh, please say it ain't so!

He laughs. "You always know when I'm speaking to you. Sometimes you have chosen to pay attention. Other times you have chosen to ignore Me."

"Me personally? I've ignored You?" Even as the words are dripping from my lips, I realize how preposterous my question is. I spent years ignoring the existence of God, and when God tells me that I spent years ignoring His existence I act like that's news to me.

Here I am, having this little conversation with myself when I realize that God is laughing, and I mean *really* laughing! He seems to be having a grand old time with this one. As I ponder the possibility that God finds humor in my abject stupidity, it occurs to me that we—you, me, all humans— were put on Earth for a multitude of reasons—not the least of which is to amuse the bajeebers out of God. Judging by the deep, rich, sincerely amused laughter that I can actually feel in every nook and cranny of my body, I'm convinced that we humans definitely are God's personal Martian Floor Show.

CHAPTER 20

⬡

Just Because It's Free Doesn't Mean It Won't Cost You

S ome people live by the Golden Rule: *"Do unto others as you would have them do unto you."* Some people live by the Gilded Rule: *"He who has the gold makes the rules."* And some people live by the Gonad Rule: *"Might makes right."* Well, guess what—as it turns out, the only rule that really rules is *"he who makes his own rules is making a major mistake."*

"Man never ceases to amaze Me," He says, and just as I'm about to say *thank you* He says, "And that is *not* meant as a compliment. Regardless of how many clues I give, or how clearly I indicate My meaning, man often manages to draw all the wrong conclusions."

"Conclusions? What conclusions are You referring to?" I ask.

"I give you flowers that are beautiful to look at

and lovely to smell, and from that you conclude that I have given them to you to be plucked from the ground, crushed into powder, and injected into your body. I give you magnificent winged creatures that soar through the air, and you conclude that they were born to be caught and locked in cages. I give you majestic beasts, and you conclude that they exist so that you may cover yourself in their fur. I give you pristine oceans teeming with life. You fill them with garbage. I give you crystal-clear air. You fill it with poisons. I give you the atoms of life. You tear them in two and use them to bring death. Man has found ways to turn lies into truth, hatred into honor, and Sin into virtue. Of all the perils man has ever known—all the dangers, diseases, and disasters—none has done more damage than man himself. He is the agent of his own destruction."

God is not sounding pleased. (For the record, He's much more fun to be around when He is pleased!) Is He telling me that we've blown it? That we've already signed our own Death Certificate? That we've put the final nail in our own coffin? Are we doomed? No need to ask. He's offering the answer as I'm pondering the question.

"It is very late, but until the end is actually at hand, it is not *too* late. Man charts his own Destiny. A sailing ship will run aground if piloted into the shore, but change its course, and it will sail safely out to sea," He says.

Quick, prepare to come about. Hard to starboard. Trim the sails. Mizzen the mast. Do something! Okay, I'll do something. I'll change course. I'll return to an earlier topic. Something on a lighter note.

"The Catholic Church says that the use of birth control is a Sin. Is it?" (Okay, so it isn't a *lighter* note, but it is a note that I think needs to be played.)

He wastes no time. "Until fairly recently, the Catholic Church said that eating meat on Friday was a Sin. Please, don't get me started!"

I glance down, checking for cracks in the Vatican's foundation. I don't see any, but then, from my present vantage point, I'm not seeing much of anything, so I square my shoulders and press on. In for a penny, in for a pound, as the saying goes. Here comes the 64-thousand dollar question. "Are the Pro-Life people right? In your eyes, is abortion a Sin?"

He doesn't answer immediately, which is good because I'm not sure I'm going to like His answer. I think about covering my ears, but it won't make any difference. As I've discovered, when God wants to talk to you, He talks to you, whether you're listening or not.

"I find it interesting that the group that refers to itself as Pro-Life is opposed to the interruption of the life cycle on one end, and yet in favor of it on the other. They denounce those who practice abortion, while, at the same time, praising those who take the lives of law breakers. How is it possible to abhor one killing while advocating another?"

"Are You telling me that God is Pro-Choice?"

"Free Will implies choice," He says. "As the architect of Free Will, I am, by My very nature, Pro-Choice."

Note to self: Send condolence
card to the Pope.

"However," He continues, "that does not mean that I approve of every choice man makes. All choices beget consequences. The choice itself is up to the individual. The consequence of having made that choice is up to Me."

Note to self: Consider holding off
on that card to the Pope.

CHAPTER 21

※

Is That Your Final Question?

A little voice in my head keeps whispering that it isn't my time—I'm not supposed to be here yet. Heaven, or what tiny piece of it I've seen, seems like a lovely place, and God seems like a great guy (so to speak), but the more I think about it, the more convinced I become that the timing is all wrong. I'm not even thirty yet. In *"adult years"* I'm still just a kid. There are all kinds of things I have yet to do and places I have yet to see. The words to an old song by the rock band Traffic appear in my head: *"If you had just one minute to breathe, and they granted you one final wish, would you ask for something like another chance?"*

I find myself wondering if God issues Rain Checks, but the words that fall out of me are "Has anyone ever arrived here and been allowed to go back?"

"It has been known to happen," He explains, adding a 64-thousand-dollar question of His own, "What would be your reason for returning?"

I'm reasonably certain that not only is that *not* a rhetorical question, but, in fact, it's a question whose answer might significantly change my immediate circumstances.

I think for what seems like forever and then tell Him a number of things that He must have already known, like the fact that I haven't done much with my life other than find creative ways to mess it up. "I'd like a chance to do something meaningful," I say.

"You had a chance," He points out.

I swallow hard. He's right—of course He's right. I had a chance…and I wasted it. So, was I a candidate for a *second* chance? I didn't have a chance to ask the question about having a chance because He had a question of His own for me. "If I were to give you that second chance, what would you do with it?"

Now there's a great party question: "If you could live your life over again, knowing everything you know now, what changes would you make?" Too bad this isn't a party!

I used to tell people that if I had my life to live over again, I wouldn't do anything any differently, because if I changed *anything*, I wouldn't end up being the same person, and since I really liked the person I was, I didn't want to do anything that might change her into someone else. That was my "party answer," but the truth is that answer wasn't the truth when I spoke it at all those parties, and it certainly isn't the truth now that I've heard what

I've been hearing from the Voice of Ultimate Truth.

"If I could live my life over again," I tell Him, "I'd do all kinds of things differently, and if it ended up changing me, so much the better! I'm certainly no prize the way I am!"

Heart racing. Palms sweating.
Must. Calm. Down.

"If I let you go back, you wouldn't get to start over from the beginning. You'd only be able to pick up from where you left off," He tells me.

I'll take it. Where do I sign? I struggle to control my excitement. The last thing I want to do is insult God by turning down an invitation to move into Heaven. What about a Rain Check? Did turning down today's invitation mean that the next one might get lost in the mail? That's what I wonder and that's precisely what I ask.

"We'll see," He responds.

That involuntary shiver hits me again. "I really, really, *really* wish You'd stop saying those words."

He laughs. I shiver.

"So, can I go back? *May* I go back?" I ask.

"Would that be your final question for Me?"

My final question? I only get one more question? Will that final question determine whether or not I can go back to the *Land of the Living*? I ask Him one of those questions—which one doesn't really matter, because all He says in response is

"Is *that* your final question for God?" He chuckles. He's enjoying Himself again.

"No, that is not my final question. Is this some kind of test?"

"Is *that* your final question for God?" He's doing some serious laughing now.

"No!" I say, with only the slightest hint of childish foot stomping.

He stops laughing long enough to say, "In that case, I won't answer it."

Now I'm racking my brain. I can't think clearly. The possibility of being given a second chance at life is making my head spin. In an effort to buy time I say, "Okay, here's my final question for God. What are the real words to *Louie Louie*?" Before He has a chance to start singing, I tell Him that I was only kidding.

I clear my throat—it clears much more easily than my head. God is waiting for me to ask one more question, and it's probably not a good idea to keep God waiting, but what is that question? Is there only one question that remains to be asked? If I choose the wrong question, will He deny my request for a return visit to planet Earth? Lots of questions are swirling around in my head, but I'm pretty sure that none of them is *the* question!

I've been paying attention. *Everything* is about choices. We are free to make them. He is free to hand us the consequences. I try to remember everything He's told me—about Fate, Responsibility, Faith, Choice, Prayer. I search my brain for the one meaningful question I have yet to ask. What is that one question? I can feel my time running out. What question have I not asked? What important question has yet to occur to me? I don't know, so I do what I always do when I don't know what to do—I vamp.

"If you let me go back, I'll stop doing the really stupid things I used to do, and I'll start doing the smart things I should have been doing. In other words, I will live my life *very* differently." I stop talking and wait for His response. The wait is exceedingly brief.

"So, your final question for Me would be…what?"

Maybe He's expecting another guest at His front door, or maybe He's getting bored with me. Whatever the reason might be, I have the unmistakable feeling that I am neck deep in the land of *Now or Never*, and I have just one chance to ask one final question. But what is that one question?

And that's when it hits me. A question that has never even occurred to me before is now sitting on the tip of my tongue. It's a question I have never in my life thought to ask, but in that moment, in that place, after everything I've just been through, everything I've heard, everything I've felt, everything He's said, it's the one question I want to ask. It's the one question I *need* to ask. Questions like "*who killed JFK*" or "*how do dolphins sleep without drowning*" are of no importance to me. I don't even care what the real words to *Louie Louie* are. Suddenly, there is only one question on my mind, and in my heart. There is only one question whose answer I feel a desperate *need* to know, and I can't shake the feeling that my immediate future depends on it.

This would probably be a good time to point out that as a gambler, I make a great anything else, which is to say gambling is one of the many things for which I have absolutely no talent. But sometimes gambling is the only thing a girl can do, so I open my mouth and prepare to bet my life on one final question.

"God," I say meekly, "there is one question that I never in my life thought to ask You."

"Yes?" God says, with a hint of a grin in His amazing voice, "and that question would be…?"

I close my eyes, take one more deep breath, and, from the very bottom of my heart I say, "That question would be—what can I do for You?"

A moment passes—or is it an eternity? I hear myself take a deep breath. I open my eyes and find myself back in the *Land of the Living* (which, by the way, does not smell nearly as sweet as Heaven, but that's another story, best left for another time).

"I'm alive!" I shout. I look toward the ceiling and say to Him, "Thank you."

"You are welcome," I hear Him say in that Voice that vibrates in every cell of my body, followed by the words "I will see you later."

"Later? How much later?" I wonder aloud and then realize that I don't wonder at all. I know the answer, at which point God and I speak the words in two-part harmony, "We'll see."

EPILOGUE

Many years have passed since the events described in this book took place. Before writing about them, I had to spend time living with my newfound awareness and come to terms with the changes they brought.

When I opened my eyes to discover that I was, in fact, alive, I was overwhelmed by a combination of relief, joy, and confusion. I didn't even know what to call what had happened to me other than "dead, then not dead." Remember, the year was 1975 and the term "Near Death Experience" had not yet become the coin of the New Age realm.

Had the things I'd seen and heard been real, or were they merely the hallucinations of a dying mind? I didn't know, and I would not know for some time. In fact, it would be several months before I would have *proof* that what I had experienced *had* in fact occurred.

One evening, four months after awakening from my Heavenly experience, a friend invited me to join him at church. "Church?" I chuckled. "I'm not really the church-going type," I reminded him.

"It's not a church *service*," he explained, "it's a music concert."

Oh, a church *concert*. Well that's a house of a different color. Having nothing better to do on that particular night, I decided to go to his church concert. It was a Wednesday night. I was bored. He was cute. Pick your reason.

It was a small church in a quiet residential neighborhood a few miles south of San Francisco. A quaint and cozy little place obviously designed to accommodate several hundred worshippers, though on this night, there must have been at least a thousand people in there, and the music was not what I would have considered *typical* church music. (Not that I would know what *typical* church music was, or even if there was such a thing as typical church music, seeing as how I'd never actually been inside of a church during a typical church service. Is there even such a thing as a typical church service? I'm a Reform Jew—what do I know?)

On a small stage at the front of the church, a young man and woman played guitars and sang sweet, lovely songs—songs I'd never heard. The music was gentle, and though the place was packed, the atmosphere was peaceful. It was standing room only, so I stood, leaned against a back wall, and listened.

Less than thirty minutes into the concert, still leaning against that wall, my knees began to buckle.

With tears running down my cheeks, I found myself sliding down the wall until I was hunkering down on my heels, and I heard myself whisper, "I don't even know if You exist. All I know is that I've been calling all the shots in my life, and all I've succeeded in doing is failing. I have the Midas Touch—everything I put my hands on turns to mufflers. If You do exist, please take over for me. You couldn't possibly do any worse a job than I've done!"

I looked around, convinced that I'd just made a spectacle of myself, but I hadn't. No one had even noticed the tearful young woman now on her knees against the back wall. The concert ended, and my friend drove me home. Totally bewildered by what had just happened to me, I said nothing about it.

The following morning, I went to work—it was business as usual—with one significant exception. By lunch time, I realized that I hadn't uttered a single word of profanity all day. Not one tacky, nasty, rude, or off-color word had passed my lips, and, for me, that was a virtual impossibility, since I rarely spoke more than four words in a row without dropping in an expletive or three.

I got up, crossed the room, and studied myself in the mirror. I still looked like me, but something felt different. "Holy shhhiii…" I stammered, but that's as far as I got. The rest of the word would not come out of my mouth. It felt as if an Angel was grabbing my tongue. *An Angel was grabbing my tongue*—did I just think that?

Getting dizzy. Head spinning. Must sit down.

I closed my eyes, and in a flash, it all came rushing back to me. The tunnel. The light. The Voice. Oh my God! It wasn't a dream. It really happened! The woman He had described, the one who had invited Him into her life even though she didn't really believe He existed—the woman who, prior to that moment, had been incapable of uttering a sentence without filling it with rude words—that woman was *me*. He had told me about an event in my life that hadn't yet occurred. He had described a moment in my future—and it had just happened.

Getting dizzier.

I ran it all through my head—His words, my actions—and I recalled the conversation we'd had about Fate. "I gave the human race Free Will," He had told me, "and with it, you may choose your own actions. I do, however, know which choices you will make."

It wasn't Fate that all of this would happen to me. I *chose* to attend that concert the night before. I *chose* to cry out to Him, and He *chose* to make His presence known to me in a way that I could not possibly miss. I needed an aspirin!

Several decades have come and gone since the day *an Angel grabbed my tongue*, but in all that time

I have never begun a day without asking God what I can do for Him.

When I first realized that my Heavenly experience had been real, and not something my imagination had invented, one of the first things I grappled with was why, as I stood there in the presence of the greatest power ever conceived, I didn't roll myself into a fetal position, cover my eyes and ears and whimper incoherently. In fact, I was not the least bit frightened. Given the situation, shouldn't I have been? And shouldn't He have been aloof? Commanding? Terrifying? But He wasn't any of those things. What He was was comforting, compassionate, gentle and humane. In fact, He seemed downright Human!

I've given a great deal of thought to this seeming incongruity. The wrathful God of the Bible vs. the sweet, gentle, funny God of my experience. As I pondered the apparent polar opposites of those two 'beings', the phrase '*made in His image*' popped into my head.

After considerable reflection, I concluded that the '*image*' referred to in that phrase has nothing to do with physical appearances. After all, though I had spent time with Him, I had not actually *seen* Him, and He had told me that He is not a *physical being*. From that I concluded that the phrase "*made in His image*" has more to do with his *essence* than with his physique, and, being the loving, compassionate Creator of life that He is, He had chosen to meet me on *my* level because I couldn't possibly meet Him on His!

Perhaps He presented Himself to me in the manner He did because making me feel safe and comfortable is something any loving father would do. That certainly would explain why I wasn't terrified, and why He felt to me like a loving father, rather than a terrifying, vengeful King of Kings. He is God, after all, so acting the role of a loving father wouldn't be difficult for Him. If Robin Williams could do it, certainly God could do it!

That's the conclusion I have reached, and nothing has happened in all the years between then and now to make me doubt that conclusion.

Over the years, I've learned that having God in my life does not guarantee a problem-free existence. Far from it! It does, however, mean that no matter how painful, difficult, or frightening things in my life may become, I know that I need not face them on my own. Thanks to the twists and turns my life has taken, that knowledge has been given more than ample opportunity to be tested.

Not long ago, I was diagnosed with Stage 3+ Breast Cancer. When I received the diagnosis, rather than crying "Why me?" and coming completely unglued, as many who hear the words "you have Cancer" often do, I remained remarkably calm. It wasn't a calm born of denial. Quite the opposite. It was a calm born of the absolute certainty that no matter what the future had in store for me, God (or Ichabod, or Ishkabibble, or whatever you want to call Him/Her) would be right there with me, every step of the way, and He has been.

He was with me during my mastectomy. He was with me throughout my eighteen months of Chemotherapy and Radiation treaments. He was with me every time I put my face in a toilet bowl and vented my breakfast, and my lunch, and my dinner. He was with me through all of it. My Cancer is in remission now, but He's still with me, and I believe He always will be!

Sometimes I hear Him laughing *with* me. Sometimes I hear Him laughing *at* me. Apparently, making God laugh is something I keep getting better at, because with every passing day, I hear Him laughing more than He did the day before. At this rate, I could end up giving God a hernia before my time here is at an end. (Hey, with God *nothing* is impossible!)

ACKNOWLEDGMENTS

My sincere appreciation to the wonderful women of Luminare Press. To the best of my knowledge, despite my egregious refusal to abide by industry-standard rules of punctuation, not one of them (the ladies, not the punctuation rules) has been seen burning life-size effigies of yours truly (at least not yet). Thanks also to the Voice King of the Gaming World, Dave "Fenotanny" Fennoy who, when offered the role of the Voice of God in the Stage version of "Why Are There Monkeys?" was heard to say *"I've waited my entire life to hear a woman call me God!"*. Much is owed to David Ivester who, ably assisted by his buddy, Buddy, found innumerable ways to give wings to my "Monkeys..." (and, as any sage and seasoned woman can tell you, a snarky Crone with flying monkeys is a glorious and formidable force of nature).

ABOUT THE AUTHOR

To the casual observer, it appeared that Brooke Jones spent many years in tiny rooms, talking to herself. The truth is, she was talking to a few gazillion people, first in San Francisco and then in Los Angeles, via an alphabet soup of radio stations. A long and rather unpleasant battle with Breast Cancer put an end to that career. Though the price of her victory over Cancer included the loss of her bodacious TaTa's, her sense of humor remained intact. Immediately after her Mastectomy on December 23, 2005, Brooke created a Meme that said: I told Santa that all I wanted for Christmas was a pair of Boobs. And there they were, under my tree on Christmas morning – Rush Limbaugh and George W. Bush.

When she isn't creating satiric Memes for her Camp Meme-A-Day Facebook site, or writing articles for her Blog, "What If?" (www.Whatif.blog), she's creating new cards for her admittedly-twisted greeting card company, CardBard Greetings, available online in THE CARD OUTLET (www.zazzle.com/thecardoutlet).

Brooke currently resides in the relatively sane

Pacific Northwest with one loveable Golden Retriever, one miniature facsimile of a dog of dubious lineage, one soon-to-be grown orange kitten (whose name may or may not be Midget, or Munchkin, or Lady Marmalade), and the tree-hugging, guitar-playing, harp-blowing, singer-songwriter love of her life. (Brooke's, not the kitten's).

Brooke donates a portion of ALL proceeds from the sale of this book as well as the sale of all merchandise in THE CARD OUTLET to The Breast Cancer Research Foundation.

CPSIA information can be obtained
at www.ICGtesting.com
Printed in the USA
BVHW070221110522
636630BV00011B/1122

9 781643 884646